The Divine Image

Keith Ward

The Divine Image

The Foundations of Christian Morality

London
SPCK

First published 1976
SPCK
Holy Trinity Church
Marylebone Road, London NW1 4DU

© Keith Ward 1976

Printed in Great Britain by
Northumberland Press Limited
Gateshead

ISBN 0 281 02935 0

Contents

Introduction

In the latter half of the twentieth century in the western world, many people are puzzled and confused about moral issues. Sometimes, old and secure values seem to be under attack and many people no longer feel that they know what is right or wrong in matters of sexual conduct, social justice, matters of life and death, or violence as a means of political action. In a world of rapid change and uncertainty, one sometimes hears the call for a return to Christian morality; and yet Christians often seem just as confused as everyone else. Some Christians stick to the old, simple yet hard rules: no homosexuality, no sex before marriage, no contraception or abortion, no killing under any circumstances. Yet other Christians seem to have a more lax or perhaps more liberal attitude to the rules and to hold more radical moral views. What, then, after all, is the Christian attitude to moral questions? Is there just one? Does the Christian faith provide firm moral guide-lines on to which to hold in a time of confusion?

These questions raise a still more basic issue, though it is not one which is always thought of. But it is an issue which is really the most important of all: namely, upon what are one's moral opinions really based? How can one find out what is right or wrong with certainty? Have our moral beliefs got a firm basis? What are the foundations of morality? If Christians are going to have a clear and firm stand on moral issues, they must be able to answer this question. They must be able to say what the foundation of Christian morality is, what its basic principles are, and how they can be known. This book is an attempt to answer these questions, to lay the foundation for a clear Christian response to the moral problems which face us and—what is just as important—to show just where, and why, some problems can have no clear solution, even for Christians.

In our world, people maintain many different views about the foundations of morality. Some say that moral rules are just products of biological or social conditioning; they therefore vary from one culture or race to another and are not very important; they are rather like rules of etiquette, and no one set of rules is better or worse than any other. Other people say that your morality is just the way you decide to live; so again, it can vary from one person to another, and from one place or time to another. Yet others say that moral rules are just conventions to preserve a more or less secure society. A Christian cannot be content with any of these views, however much partial truth they may contain. For he believes that moral rules are based on the will of God, which is changeless and absolute. This Christian view is attacked by many non-Christians as senseless or even immoral; and many Christians are not quite sure what it means or to what it commits them in practice. So one thing I want to try to do is to show how morality can be founded on the will of God; and to argue that this does not lead to a morality of blind obedience to some absolute tyrant, but demands a sensitive, reflective, and creative response to God and to his creation.

But what are the basic principles of Christian morality? Some people say that there is only one principle, the principle of love; others hold that some acts are absolutely prohibited to man, always and everywhere. Can we formulate a set of basic Christian moral principles? In this book, I try to set out in a fairly systematic way the basic principles of Christian morality, the principles which we must take into account when we are faced with specific moral problems.

Finally, there is the question, how are we to set about making moral decisions? Do we look at the Bible, or go to the Church, or rely on our emotions, or what? In answering this question, I suggest a way of making moral decisions which takes into account both the revelation of God in

Christ and the general divine command to use our reason and experience to discover his will in the created world.

What I have not done is to tackle specific moral problems, like abortion or war or justice in society, and suggest Christian answers to them. But I have supplied the necessary materials for tackling such problems; and the personal effort of applying the principles to particular cases is perhaps the best way of coming to appreciate the difficulty and challenge of many of the moral problems our society faces, and the best way of learning to understand Christian ethics.

This book, then, expounds and argues for a specifically and distinctively Christian foundation for morality. It proposes a systematic list of basic Christian moral principles and suggests rules for ordering and applying them. It recommends a particular understanding of the Christian moral life, a way of living such that faith works out in action. The book contains discussions of Natural Law, the relation of faith and morals, the place of authority in ethics, the status of moral rules and 'absolute prohibitions', the relation of duty, happiness and purpose, and differing conceptions of 'the will of God'. It thus covers most of the ground of Moral Theology and Christian Ethics courses, and is in fact largely based on my own lectures in London and Cambridge Universities. However, it is not written merely for the academic reader, but for all who take an interest in the crucial problems of morality and in the question of how to relate faith to action.

It is worth noting that I have kept references to historical and literary sources to a bare minimum; I wish the argument to stand on its own merits, not on the record of my researches. Nevertheless, an informal bibliography of relevant literature is appended, which should enable the reader to follow up subjects in which he is interested.

'IF FAITH DOES NOT LEAD TO ACTION,
IT IS IN ITSELF A LIFELESS THING'
(James 2.17)

1

The Will of God

The Christian sees morality as a matter of obedience to the will of God. In saying this, one is not saying that there is a set of moral rules which Christians, and only Christians, must accept. The Christian may agree with a non-Christian about all his moral rules, about the sort of thing that he believes to be right or wrong. Neither is one saying that Christians have a special privileged access, in revelation, to knowledge of moral truths, which is denied to other men. Christians may agree with non-Christians about the way in which they come to believe or decide that certain things are right or wrong. What one is saying is that when a Christian says he ought to do something, that it is his duty, he means that it is God's will, which he must obey. This is a distinctive and characteristic view of what morality is; and it is the view which I am concerned to expound. I wish to show what it means and what its consequences are, to remove various misunderstandings of it, and answer various objections to it; and in this way to elucidate what I believe to be the correct and enduring foundation for Christian morality.

The three questions which I have just distinguished are importantly different from each other, although they are sometimes confused. They are: 1. What sorts of thing are right and wrong? 2. How can one tell what is right or wrong? 3. What does one mean when one says that something is morally right or wrong? The questions are closely related to each other, and probably the answer one gives to one question will influence the answer one gives the others. Nevertheless, they are different and should be considered separately. I am primarily interested in the third question, though I will in fact deal with them all, and show how they inter-relate; and my answer to the third question is that when a Christian says that something is morally right, he means that God wills it, so that he must obey.

There are many people who would immediately object to this assertion. The concept of 'obedience' may be regarded as infantile and even perverse, especially in matters of morality, leading to the horrors of Auschwitz or the Inquisition, perhaps. Talk about 'God's will', it may be said, leads to a notion of 'absolute duty' which again is pathological and dangerous, for the similar reason that it leads to unthinking action which rejects any call for justification. In any case, how can one discover what God's will actually is? Why should one obey it anyway? And cannot morality exist perfectly well without recourse to the concept of God, which is itself obscure and possibly incoherent?

One may not be surprised that atheists cannot accept the Christian view of morality, but it is perhaps painful that they actually seem to find it infantile and degrading. It may seem surprising, too, that many Christians have accepted the secular estimate and attempt to conform their view to what non-Christians require. My response to the secular challenge is a different one; while taking into account the various objections raised, I shall try to preserve and even stress the distinctiveness of the Christian view. For I believe that this may turn out to be a matter of some importance at this rather critical juncture of human history. One should not underestimate the degree to which morality itself, in any sense similar to the Christian view of it, is under attack. For one who believes that the Christian view is true, and that morality matters more than anything else in human life, this is of immense consequence. Nowhere is it more important to arrive at a just estimate of what is true and false than in morality, and that is the justification for this kind of study.

For a Christian, duty is regarded as God's will, but it needs to be said at once that there are many different interpretations possible of this statement. There are many different accounts of the nature of the will of God, of how it is relevant to moral situations, and how it can be known by men. For example, traditional Catholic theology, influenced by Thomas Aquinas, constructs a doctrine of God which is basically derived from Aristotle's ideas of a perfect, immutable, 'self-thinking thought'. God is perfect being, pure actuality, in which there is no potential or unrealized being at all, and he contains all perfections in himself in a unique and incomparable way. The will of God, on such a view, is strictly speaking identical with the being of God, though our finite minds may need to think of it as different, and, as such, it is necessarily what it is, since the being of God is necessary, and contains no contingency, or merely accidental detail, at all. So the will of God is conceived as an unchanging, necessarily fixed, and essential part of God, the eternal and immutable reality. As such, it is necessarily manifested in all his creation, in the form of a set of necessary, intelligible principles, which help to constitute the being of all things.

There are two very significant corollaries of this view for ethics. First, there is no real distinction between being and goodness; in so far as something is what it properly is, by nature, it is good; for all created things reflect the perfections of God's being in some way. Secondly, what we call ethical principles are natural principles which govern the very being of creatures; they are not somehow imposed in an arbitrary way upon a morally neutral nature. Therefore traditional Catholic moral theology tends to think of morality as a matter of discovering how to fulfil one's natural or proper human nature, and of moral principles as founded in the natural order of created things, as a 'Natural Law' which is implicit in the very idea of the rational ordering of nature to its proper end, which is the work of the Creator. The natural law of creatures reflects the eternal law of God, governing his creation of the world. The moral life will then consist in discovering one's natural inclinations and ordering them rationally, in accordance with the natural law of human behaviour, so as to arrive at their proper end. The proper end of human nature can be found by reason by a consideration of that nature, and morality consists in its implementation, according to rational, ordered principles. The two main ideas which remain embedded in this conception of the moral life are, first, that moral principles are founded in nature, and not in arbitrary personal or social decisions; and second, that nature, as the creation of a perfect being, aims at an end, so that there is a purpose of human nature, as such, which can be discovered by right reason. On this Catholic view, to say that one's duty is the will of God is more frequently expressed by saying that the principles of human action are discoverable by reason in the natural inclination of all things towards their proper fulfilment, which in turn is founded on the creative act of an intelligible and perfect creator. We discover our duty by discovering the fulfilment of our natural inclinations as men, and to aim at such fulfilment is to do the will of God, as expressed in the necessary and intelligible principles which underlie the whole of creation.

This whole Catholic world of thought is apt to seem quite alien to Protestant moralists. Perhaps the underlying reason for this is the Protestant rejection of any philosophy, even Aristotle's, as a basis for Christian thinking, and an attempted return to what were believed to be biblical categories of thought. One then begins a study of morality by referring back to the Torah, the 613 precepts of God which were, by tradition, revealed to Moses in the wilderness, and which Christians often telescope into 'the Ten Commandments'. Here we have a series of commands and prohibitions which are absolute and universal. They are commanded by divine revelation, and are backed up by sanctions and by rewards and punishments, to be visited by God upon his people. They are not worked out by human reason. Indeed, to this day no one has ever been able to give a rational explanation for all the food and purity rituals of the Old Testament, despite the attempts of modern critics to see them as early public health regulations. Furthermore, what we would call moral and ritual laws are mixed up together without any clear distinction; all are equally commands of God, simply to be obeyed by men, not to be questioned. The model of God used here is the Old Testament concept of an omnipotent sheikh or tribal chief who hands down his laws at will and commands instant obedience on pain of death. Man must obey the unfathomable decrees of an absolute omnipotent creator; before them, creatures can only bow in submission. One's duty is to do what God commands, to keep the Law he has revealed.

The Christian understanding modifies this Old Testament account by the Pauline insistence that faith frees us from the Law, or at least from its ritual prescriptions; but Jesus takes the place of Moses as the one who reveals human duty, especially in the Sermon on the Mount, in Matthew 5–7. And just as Jews often saw the Torah as the almost personal Wisdom of God, given as a revealed way of life for men to delight in and love intensely; so Christians see Jesus as the Word of God, showing in his own life a pattern for all men to love and delight in. On this understanding, the authority of revelation has a very high place; and there is a relatively sharp distinction between the community to which revelation is given—the chosen people, the true Church—and those outside, who do not have the revealed Law to treasure and observe.

Protestants who take a more radical view of the biblical material, and who are consequently unable to accept the Torah or the words of Christ as authoritative *per se*, often preserve the notion of the will of God as a divine command issued to the redeemed community. But then they tend to see the command, not as elaborated in biblical regulations, but as directly addressed to the individual Christian in his own situation, as he stands within the community of the Church. So there are no absolute and universal commands of God; only the unique word addressed to the individual here and now. Duty cannot be specified in advance, and God's sovereign will is not bounded even by the words of the Bible, much less by Natural Law.

Some who take this general view object both to all laying-down of general ethical principles and to talk of imperatives in Christian ethics. For they would say, like Karl Barth, that God's word of salvation actually recreates man and frees him from all regulations, so that the Christian life is not so much a life of obeying moral rules as of being remade continually by God himself, a matter of indicative and not imperative, as it is sometimes put. This view is expressed very paradoxically, but the thought behind it is that God's commands are not alien orders to be obeyed out of fear but rather direct addresses of a personal and gracious God to the individual man, which when he responds in trust and faith, bring him into a new, responsible freedom.

These general interpretations roughly correspond to what LeRoy Long has called the deliberative, prescriptive, and relational motifs in Christian ethics (LeRoy Long, *A Survey of Christian Ethics*, OUP 1967). It is possible for a Christian to regard morality as a primarily deliberative matter, reflecting on human nature to discover the actions proper to man as a creature made in the image of God. Or he may view morality as fundamentally prescriptive, a matter of rules and teachings given by God, through the Bible or the Church. Or he may regard morality as basically relational, springing from the direct relation of the believer to the God by whom he is uniquely addressed. These various emphases all appear to be legitimate interpretations of the claim that one's duty is the will of God, though no one person could hold them all at the same time.

It is apparent, then, that there is not just one way of interpreting duty as God's will. First, the concept of God itself may vary from the Thomist notion of a perfect, necessary, immutable, self-sufficient being to the Reformer's notion of a free and sovereign personal will, out-flowing in love, free to interact with his creatures as he wills, and suffering to bring men to himself; or to the Process-theologians' notion of an unsurpassable being-in-process, the all-inclusive knower and lover of the world, acting in co-operation with the freedom of all finite beings; and there are other ways of conceiving God than these available. Secondly, accounts of what it is for God to have a will may differ widely. There is the Thomist notion of an immutable and intelligible structure underlying all creation; the

Reformed notion of an absolutely unconditioned divine *fiat*, which may change as it addresses individuals personally and uniquely; the Process notion of a *nisus* or tendency in the world towards the increase of value; and others too. Thirdly, there are differences about how God's will relates to the moral life. To stick to our three examples, one has the notion of morality as a following of the natural and intelligible structures of one's own being; as the unpredictable response to a direct encounter with an absolute demand; and as a creative reaching-out to new possibilities of action and value. Fourthly, there are differences as to how God's will is to be known by men; and we may think of this as the reasoned analysis of man's natural inclinations and working out of the way to achieve them; the total submission of the will before the authoritative declaration of God's redeeming word and act in Christ; and the growth into a natural life of charity and reconciliation which derives from a growing apprehension of God's love and reconciling action. In other words, one may be told to work it out for oneself by a rational study of human nature; to accept the Bible or the 'inner light' as authoritative command; or to learn God's will by the mystical path of learning union with God, and so conformity to the likeness of Christ.

I do not claim that this is an exhaustive list of ways in which duty may be, and has been, interpreted as God's will; every original theologian will bring his own nuances to the scene. This may make one think that there need really be very little in common between those who regard duty as the will of God; so that there is not much point in making this phrase the foundation of an attempt to say what is distinctive about Christian morality. But beneath this seeming plethora of interpretations, there are three basic elements which remain important and decisive in any Christian interpretation, and it is these elements which locate the distinctiveness of Christian ethics in this respect.

2

The Christian Conception of Duty

The first element which is important in the Christian interpretation of duty is that Christian faith necessitates an
attitude which may be called 'moral seriousness', that is,
moral conduct is of ultimate and decisive importance in
human life. However God is conceived in detail, Christians
always conceive him as a moral or righteous being, who
makes moral demands on his people. On some views,
morality is not really very important, since it only consists of
a set of rules or prohibitions to restrain desires where they
threaten to become anti-social. For such views, some moral
rules may be necessary; but if so, they are on the whole
unfortunate and rather minimal; restraints on conduct for
the sake of peace and good order, which have no further
intrinsic importance.

For Christians, however, moral rules, whether they are
thought to be implicit in the orders of creation or direct
commands from God, are of supreme and intrinsic importance; their positive pursuit requires sacrifice and subordination of all other interests. Man is commanded to be holy as
God is holy; to be perfect; to strive for love, humility, and
justice with all his might. Morality is an object of endeavour
and is of over-riding importance. Some Christians might
be tempted to disagree here, but the dispute would really
be a verbal, trivial one. For these Christians might say that
morality without faith is worthless; and others, in a different
tradition, might say that the pursuit of duty for its own sake
is unbalanced, since it is happiness and true well-being that
one really seeks. However, when one examines what they
go on to say about Christian living, one finds that faith itself
carries heavy ethical demands; it works itself out in a love

8

which asks for absolute commitment to the needy, poor, and outcast. Moreover to achieve the consummation of one's deepest desires in the vision of God requires a discipline and a fortitude which control the whole of one's life. So, in contrast to some religious outlooks and many non-religious accounts of morality as a social restriction on one's wants, Christianity is united in stressing that moral commitment is over-riding and covers every aspect of life, presenting a goal or demand or impetus which always calls one beyond one's present state into a wider and deeper love and endeavour. That insistent, totally demanding, and over-riding call, whether it is analytically construed as the voice of duty, the impulsion towards one's deepest fulfilment, the command of God's sovereign will or the recreative Word of divine grace, expresses the moral seriousness of the Christian life.

Secondly, that call is rooted in the objective being of God. It is not founded on some autonomous human decision or solely upon the empirically given nature of man. Since it has its foundation in the eternal decrees of the Creator, it is quite objective, independent of human belief, knowledge, or desire in the first place. Again, this objectivity may be interpreted in different ways. It may be found in the eternal laws and principles of creation, in absolute and universal rules; or it may be found in direct and situational commands of God. It does not follow from belief in objectivity that moral laws must be universal and absolute; they may change from time to time and from place to place, and still be objectively rooted in God's will. It does not follow that one has any infallible insight into what the objective moral truths are in particular cases. Indeed, it is quite consistent to hold that objective moral truths are often very difficult or even impossible to discover with certainty, even though one may claim that some rather general principles are known with a sufficiently high degree of probability to be called 'knowledge'. Nor does it necessarily follow that there is only one morally correct decision in any situation, for God's will may not be specified absolutely in every particular situation.

An example may make this point clearer. Suppose that

John Smith is a salesman, and his colleagues ask him to join with them in claiming more travelling expenses than they actually incur, a practice which, they assure him, is quite usual and taken into account by the management in fixing their bonuses. Is the morally correct thing for him to insist on total honesty, thus exposing their exaggerated claims, or to compromise for the sake of good personal relations with his colleagues? Now a moral objectivist will say that some possible courses of action are definitely ruled out, such as grossly exaggerated claims which amount to stealing, whereas some are positively enjoined: for instance, one should seriously consider the consequences of one's actions and try to aim at some increase in the general good. But the situations in which men become involved, the precise nature of one's relationships with one's colleagues, the sort of implicit understandings which underlie business practice, and so on, do vary enormously in different social groups. So there is almost certainly no one universally binding rule which applies, such as 'never be dishonest'. The morally appropriate thing to do may vary from one situation to another; in one circumstance, it may be right to insist on honesty, but in another, it may be right to accept current standards. It will depend very much on factors which cannot be completely specified in advance, about probable consequences, assessments of institutions, and probable reactions of others. Moreover, there may not be just one morally right course. Given the limitations of human foreknowledge and judgement, it may be impossible to say which act will produce the best consequences; so that one is tempted to say that the act will be morally right which expresses one's seriously considered judgement on the matter, though others, or oneself at another time, may have judged otherwise on the same available evidence.

In the case under consideration, one could simply apply a universal prohibition against dishonesty, and some people probably would. But one might say, 'You must weigh up all the factors: your friendship, the firm's practice, how others will understand your act, and so on, and decide what to do yourself. There is no one right answer waiting to be discovered. Within the range of morally permissible alternatives, you are free to decide, as long as you do so with care and love and understanding. Those are the only absolute moral principles in this situation'. A theist who took the former view would conceive God's will as laid down in absolute prohibitions, to be applied rigorously to conduct. But a theist who took the latter view would conceive of God as laying down general directives for moral action— 'act with love', 'seek understanding'—and as laying down the parameters, the limits, of permissible action—'do not steal'; 'do not undermine trust'—but as leaving creatures free to decide exactly how to act according to these methods and within these limits; and, no doubt, to learn from that use of freedom.

Therefore to say that morality is rooted in the being of God does not at all commit one to a view of a number of absolute and universal moral rules, laid up in heaven, which men must simply apply automatically, like a computer, as they come up. But it does commit one to saying that there are definite moral truths, whatever human beliefs and desires are, which one must seek to apprehend correctly. Just as the world of tables and chairs exists independently— so most would say—and is to be understood by us, so there are independently existing aspects of being which give rise to moral obligations, and which can be understood by us. Morality is not, in other words, a matter of human decision, taste, or emotion, for which there is no correct and incorrect, no understanding to be won, nor error to be avoided. In morality, as in the sciences, one can progress and learn. What has been spoken of as the 'over-riding call' of morality can be known and responded to more and more fully; to be moral is to respond emotionally, volitionally, and cognitively to the reality of God.

There are those, especially in the Catholic tradition, who would still be suspicious of this rather Platonic-sounding view of Christian morality as a growing into greater knowledge of God as the one in whom moral demands are rooted. For they might prefer to think of morality more prosaically, as the means to human flourishing, and as thus founded, after all, on human desires and their fulfilment. But, of course, they would not deny that there is a God, that God has created human desires and the conditions of their fulfilment, and that true fulfilment can be found only in union with God. The subjective end of human action may be happiness, but the objective end, that which alone brings supreme happiness, is God himself. For a Christian, the view that good action consists in the fulfilment of natural human inclinations and propensities must be complemented by the recognition that true human fulfilment is found in response to God; and God's reality is acknowledged not just by a theoretical assent, but by a submission of will to his supreme perfection.

Similarly, the tradition of liberal Protestantism which has been influenced by the allegedly Kantian ethic of 'duty for duty's sake', and which stresses above all the absolute demand of the ethical, needs to recognize that it is precisely in response to God's call that human fulfilment is realized. So moral action is not a-rational obedience, but an obedience founded on the rationality of God the Creator, who wills the fulfilment of all his creatures. The Catholic tradition has neglected, in theory, the element of duty—maybe because there was simply no word for duty in Aristotle's Greek—as a category of ultimate importance, and some Protestant traditions have neglected, in theory, the rationality of the moral life and its integral connection to human flourishing. But both traditions agree that ethics is objective, in that human moral action arises as a response to a reality, however conceived, which demands human submission and a progressive learning of obedience along with a growth in knowledge of the reality with which we continually interact.

The Christian not only takes morality with an ultimate seriousness, and grounds it in an objective reality to which man is called to respond creatively. The third element which is important in the Christian interpretation of duty is that it is located in a 'will'. Morality is not only objective; it is somehow personalistic, for the theist; it belongs to a category conceived by analogy with personal interactions in society.

12

As such, it is opposed to objectivist accounts of morality which think of the objective moral order as impersonal or non-purposive. For instance, the English philosopher G. E. Moore was an objectivist, but construed the objective realities upon which morality is founded as special, 'non-natural' properties of goodness, though the status of these properties remains very obscure; and W. D. Ross held that there simply exist certain self-evidently true moral propositions, which can be intuited by men. Philosophers have always felt uneasy about these moral properties or propositions, which seem to dangle about in the universe in a strange incoherent way. Some Indian religious accounts of morality, too, seem to conceive it impersonally, as a sort of cosmic law of right, a law which does not lead to any goal but simply expresses the morally ordered nature of a basically purposeless, even illusory, universe.

In opposition to such accounts, Christianity relates morality to a personal will and purpose. It is characteristic of Semitic religion that moral principles are regarded as divine commands, on the analogy of a king or sheikh ordering his subjects to do what he desires. This can lead, on the one hand, to God being conceived as a tyrannical and arbitrary despot, cowing his subjects into obedience, on the other to man regarding moral principles as expressions of a purpose in the created order, which will fulfil the goals of a personalistically conceived Creator. Men can then be regarded as co-operating freely with this purpose, out of love and a desire for a closer personal relationship to the Creator. When one speaks of a divine will, it is this sense of human co-operation with a larger cosmic purpose which is most important, and that purpose is a fully self-conscious one; not some sort of blind cosmic striving to a final consummation, but a fully intentional driving and sustaining power behind all created things. Furthermore, it is a purpose which issues in an enlarging of personal, as opposed to impersonal, reality; a goal which we conceive dimly under the name of love. The Christian envisages the universe as purposively ordered towards a growth in perfect love; and thus as both beginning from and ending in a fully personal reality—or, to take analogy seriously, a reality which cannot be less than personal. The moral life of the Christian basically consists in the free and creative response to this personal reality and a free co-operation in working out his purposes of love.

If I may again attack positions which are indeed oversimplified, but which help me to make my positive points, one can say that the traditional Catholic moral theology rightly stressed the element of purpose in ethics, by speaking of man's proper end; but it has tended somehow to make these purposes impersonal or subpersonal purposes of Nature as an autonomous reality, rather than purposes of a God beyond nature, to whom response must be made. For example, some traditional prohibitions of contraception rely on the notion of purposes of nature in the sexual act, considered as an autonomous biological reality, which must not be tampered with by man, but they say little about the calling of man into fuller personal relationships, within which sexual acts are transformed and re-orientated.

Some Protestant traditions, on the other hand, have tended to undermine the freedom and creativity of human response by tying morality up in a strict and exhaustive set of rules for living; or they have stressed the sovereignty and absoluteness of the divine imperative to such an extent that any notion of a rational purpose in the created order, to be worked out in society as well as in personal life, has virtually disappeared. Categorical rules have ousted the notion of a proper end and goal for man from some Protestant accounts of ethics; and so the 'natural man' becomes a fallen, totally depraved creature, and God's commands come, not to show him his possible goal, but solely to convict him of sin and to discipline his unruly will. As against these positions, oversimplified here, and no doubt unrepresentative of the best in Catholic and Protestant thought, one must stress that the divine purpose is being worked out in nature; but that it is a fully personal purpose, which requires of man a fully personal response, and thus leaves him a great measure of free decision in making that response.

So far I have suggested that, while there are many different interpretations of morality within Christianity, there are nevertheless three common elements which mark out as distinctive a Christian conception of duty. Those are: 1. A moral seriousness which makes moral norms of ultimate, not merely subsidiary concern; 2. A commitment to objectivity which stresses that morality is a matter of response, not decision or sentiment; 3. An interpretation of morality in terms of a fully personal purpose in the universe, with which man is called to co-operate in his moral life. These elements are aptly summed up in the assertion that, for a Christian, duty is the will of God.

There is, then, a distinctive Christian conception of duty but does it really in practice make any difference? It may sound different, but in daily living, what difference does it really make? That is the question with which I will deal now, in going on to interpret more specifically the three elements I have mentioned within the Christian conception of duty.

3

Moral Seriousness

What difference does it make to believe in moral seriousness? This is a matter of one's general attitude to morality,
one's way of regarding all moral issues, rather than the
addition of any specific moral principle to an already existing list. What it decrees is taking some matters very seriously,
as of over-riding importance. It means that one will, or
should, take time to consider what one should do, try to
take all relevant factors into consideration, and decide
responsibly and in full knowledge of what one is doing. It
specifies a method of making moral decisions. This means
that it may well lead to a difference in one's actual moral
principles from those of an unreflective or morally frivolous
person; action after conscious deliberation and choice may
well be very different from unreflective or spontaneous
action. But one cannot say in advance just what these
differences might be, or whether there will necessarily be
any, in a specific case. One should remember that morality
is not simply a matter of a list of principles, existing in a
vacuum. It is a matter of personal beings deciding how to
act; so there is a great moral difference between a person
who decides reflectively, with a concern for the good, and
a person who just follows inclination or social convention.
This is the sort of difference some existentialists were no
doubt trying to sketch in making the distinction between
'authentic' and 'inauthentic' living, between acting in conscious acceptance of one's freedom and responsibility, and
just acting naturally, as one of the crowd.

Moral seriousness, then, makes a great difference in one's
daily living; for it makes a difference to the sort of person
one is and the way one makes one's decisions about acting.

16

There is a point of fundamental importance here. I am saying that moral agreement is not simply agreement in moral principles. Far from it; the deepest level of moral agreement is agreement about the sort of person one should be and the understanding of human action one has; and this is in fact compatible with disagreement about particular moral principles. Kant pointed out how a man could subscribe to the principle of fair trade from a variety of motives: from self-interest, seeing that fair trade is good for business; from inclination, just because he is a naturally fair person; or from duty, because it is the way he ought to act. So, Kant said, there is a very great difference between acting in accordance with duty, with the principle which states what one ought to do, and acting *from* duty, or doing a thing because it is your duty. Kant wrote that the only unconditionally good thing in the whole world was the 'good will', the intention of a man to do something simply because it is his duty, to do a thing for the sake of duty.

This principle of Kant's has, I think, been very much misunderstood, though this is not the place to go too deeply into the matter. I will confine myself to saying that he did not mean that every time a person performs an action, he has to think consciously, 'this is my duty'; indeed, he christens the sort of man who consciously thinks of nothing but duty all the time a moral fanatic. Moreover, Kant makes the point that our innermost motives are so mixed, most of the time, that we cannot even be certain what they are. Kant's view is that the morally good man will indeed always act from the motive of duty, but this will not be a conscious and laborious thinking about it; it will be a habitual disposition to do certain things simply because they ought to be done. Dutifulness—which is just what I have called moral seriousness—is a general, and largely unconscious, disposition according to which a man acts. Often we will say that a certain person is an ambitious person; and we do not mean that he thinks he is ambitious, and always asks himself what the ambitious thing to do is. In fact, he may be the last person to admit that he is ambitious. What we mean is that he always does things which show that his innermost desire

17

—whether or not he admits it—is to achieve power or pre-eminence. Similarly, we can speak of a dutiful person; and we need not mean that he thinks he is dutiful, or that he always asks himself what his duty is, or that he is constantly exhorting himself to obey the demands of duty. We may mean simply that he always does things in a way which shows that his innermost orientation is to be just, temperate, prudent, and loving, not out of self-interest, but for their own sake. Just as the self-interested person will consistently act out of self-interest in whatever he does, without necessarily asking himself what the self-interested thing to do will be; so the dutiful person will consistently refrain from immoral acts and perform his obligations at all times, without necessarily asking himself what his duty is, and exhorting himself to do it. Basically, the dutiful or morally serious person is one who is disposed to act with prudence and care, to discover the sort of thing that ought to be done, and to do it for no other reason than that.

Moral seriousness, then, makes a difference to the way one goes about making practical decisions. It may not add any distinctive moral principles to an already existent list, but it does enjoin one to consider seriously the sorts of action which men should perform or from which they should refrain, and to follow the dictates of morality even in opposition to inclinations and interests (if there is a conflict, which there often need not be). These injunctions can be usefully codified in the traditional list of 'cardinal virtues', which have been handed down from the ancient Greeks. These are the virtues of wisdom (or prudence); courage (or fortitude); temperance (or self-control) and justice. They are called cardinal virtues, because they have been thought to be the basic virtues, in terms of which all other virtues can be analysed or explained. That is almost certainly not the case; for instance, neither love nor humility, both important Christian virtues, can be derived from the list. The truth is that these four virtues just formed a traditional list in Greece, and as such, were taken over and discussed by Plato and Aristotle, thus passing into the Christian tradition also. Nevertheless, the list is useful for clarifying what is involved in being morally serious.

The virtue of prudence counsels against thoughtlessness in conduct. To discover how one should act in a very complex and uncertain world requires many intellectual skills. One needs to know all the facts of the case; to see the probable consequences of one's actions; to decide the most effective means to the ends one desires; to see how general principles can be applied in particular cases; and to weigh various factors which may well be divergent. Moral decision-making is not at all a straightforward undertaking; the Christian has no special direct intuition which tells him infallibly what he should do. Reason and judgement must both be used in the laborious and rather uncertain process of deciding what it is that one should do in particular cases. It is important to see that using reason is not a matter of mechanical calculation or deduction; the human use of reason involves the ability to disentangle important from unimportant features of the case, sensitivity to all the various factors involved, and the capacity to relate various principles and adapt them to new cases. In a word, the human use of reason involves insight, the grasp of relationships and priorities, to which the work of deduction and inference is only an aid. Just as there is no infallible intuition of ethical truth, so there is no mechanical procedure for calculating what ought to be done. The laborious work of reason, analysing factors and projecting consequences, and the hesitant groping for insight into those factors, work together in coming to a moral decision. To be morally serious is to take thought about one's decisions and choices; and that involves the virtue of wisdom or prudence, the virtue of reason judiciously and carefully applied.

The virtue of justice counsels against partiality in conduct. It is only too easy to put oneself or one's own group first, and to leave others to take care of themselves, but it is part of morality to consider equally all persons involved in a particular decision, and to be sensitive to their needs and desires. This can be accomplished by generalization from the particular case to provide a principle which one is prepared to apply to anyone in a similar situation. This is not a technique for providing one infallible rule of justice; there may be many disputes about which impartial principles one should espouse. But at least to aim at impartiality and equality of consideration and to say that one is prepared to be treated as one treats others, is a requirement of the moral point of view. To be morally serious is to consider the needs and desires of others equally with one's own and to act on principles which one is prepared to see applied both to oneself and others; and that involves the virtue of justice, the impartial generalization of one's principles of action.

The virtue of fortitude counsels against the relaxation of moral endeavour in face of threat or difficulty or opposition. Courage is the disposition to overcome fear in face of danger, for a good cause. In morality, it includes the preparedness to stand up for one's principles, even in difficult conditions. Courage is sometimes thought to be a martial virtue or the heroic virtue of being prepared to die for one's principles. It can certainly include that, but it is also much wider in scope. For it covers the sort of resolution or 'staying-power' that can make a man continue to stand by moral principles, even when he is weakened or disheartened, or when his fellows are indifferent or opposed to his views. Fortitude can be a very annoying virtue, of course; when it is possessed by those whose views differ markedly from our own, we call it stubbornness, and one must be careful that, in standing by one's principles, one is not simply being intolerant and stubborn. Nevertheless, to be morally serious is to regard some principles as so important that one must defend and live by them in face of any amount of mockery or threat; and that involves the virtue of fortitude, the resolution of reason in face of danger and difficulty.

The virtue of temperance counsels against the subordination of moral principles to passions and inclinations. Human desires are very strong; and while they are not in themselves wrong, they are strong enough to upset any intended course of human action. It is when our desires take control and prevent us from implementing our moral principles that they are dangerous and immoral. To have the virtue of temperance is to be able to control one's whims and desires, such as sexuality, hunger, anger, jealousy, and greed by conforming them to moral principles. The desires are not simply to be exterminated but they are to be controlled and brought into line with moral principles. To be morally serious is to control one's desires and feelings so that they do not impede, but rather help to promote, the ends of morality. It is to refuse to let one's desires control one's life, seeking their immediate gratification without regard for moral concerns. This is not just to repress them, but to seek to use them positively in the pursuit of moral aims, such as, to extend one's natural feelings of sympathy and to direct one's anger against injustice and oppression. This is the virtue of temperance, the moderation and direction of the passions by reason.

The four cardinal virtues, then, represent the triumph of reason over thoughtlessness, partiality, threat, and passion. To outline these virtues is not to tell one specifically what is to be done or what precise moral principles one should espouse. It is rather to show the sort of person one must be if one is to take morality seriously. In all this, it is presupposed that there are principles which should be taken seriously, as of ultimate importance, and which should be implemented for their own sake; and it has been suggested that rationality plays a very large part in determining what these principles are and in sustaining and applying them. But even though we have not been able to outline the set of Christian moral principles as yet, we are now able to say what character the morally serious man will have. He will be thoughtful, dispassionate, calm and self-possessed; he will give a high place to rationality in his account of human nature; and he will regard those principles which he takes to be moral as over-riding any non-moral principles and as worth implementing, not for any further reason, but for their own sake. There is certainly a definite and distinctive attitude to morality here; its accounts of human nature and virtues and of the ultimate ends of human action would be actively denied by many. This attitude makes a

4

Objectivity

The second main element in the Christian conception of duty is the commitment to objectivity. What difference does it make to believe in an objective moral order? The importance of such a belief again lies not in adding new principles to a given list, but in the way one goes about making practical decisions in one's life. The person who attributes objectivity to morality is one who believes that the moral life is one of response to a reality outside himself; that he can learn and grow in knowledge; that he can be mistaken; that some moral views are more correct than others. Morality is not just a matter of decision or of doing what one most wants in the long term. It is a matter of discovering and responding, knowing and learning; ultimately, for the Christian, a growth in the knowledge and love of God.

There are many ways of misconstruing the nature of this moral response. One may see it as the acceptance on authority of a set of rules or commands; but this makes morality into something external, imposed on man from without, repressing his own nature; and it dehumanises the character of the response, making it a mechanical process of transcription of rule into conduct, which a computer could do better. Another misconception of objectivity is that one intuits immediately, either in the particular situation or in general, some clear moral rule which one must then put into effect. If that were the case, morality might be much clearer and less ambiguous, but the elements of judgement, insight, decision, and creativity which, for all the good or ill they entail, make persons what they are, would be totally missing. Morality, and so human life, would be very different from what it actually is. Perhaps the quality which most basically characterizes the moral response could be called sensitivity, receptivity, or openness. It lies in a preparedness to be affected by one's particular situation and to respond to all the factors in that situation without partiality or pre-judgement. It lies in the resolution to see things as they really are; to extend and clarify one's vision; to respond fully and appropriately; and to make one's actions appropriate responses to what one sees. For the objectivist, morality runs out into contemplation; and an essential part of the moral quest is the clearing and quieting of the mind which may give one an undistorted vision and a measured response. The acceptance and application of moral principles without the contemplative insight upon which they are properly founded can give rise to a rigorous legalism, in which rigid laws are applied without sensitivity. But it is also possible for contemplation so to dominate one's life that one never actually gets around to making any response in action. What one needs is a responsiveness which is both fully appreciative and which leads to action; and that is the attitude the objectivist aims to adopt.

One might say that this is the virtue of love; but if so, it is love interpreted in a very wide sense. It is love considered as sympathetic appreciation of all one's experiences, and appropriate action in response. There are many sorts of situations and experiences in the world, not all of them delightful or valuable by any means. One may respond with delight to a beautiful view or to the physical world with wonder and curiosity or to people with concern or to the infliction of suffering on others with revulsion. It is fitting to speak of some of these as appropriate objects of contemplation, but one may shrink from contemplating an act of torture, for example. There are, however, Buddhist meditations on suffering, sorrow, and death; and perhaps one should not shrink from exploring these aspects of reality, too, if only to come to a true view of the pain and transitoriness of the world. There is pain, evil, loss, and death in our world, and while one can hardly be said to savour them appreciatively, perhaps one should be sensitive

24

to them and seek to understand their nature.

How will the cultivation of such general sensitivity affect morality? Well, the point of such contemplation is that it should issue in appropriate action, and that one's action should be in response to what one perceives. The appropriate response to beauty may be simply to savour it, or it may be to learn to paint or assess it by learning critical techniques. The appropriate response to the contemplation of death may be to renew one's understanding of life as finite and transitory. The appropriate response to the suffering of another person may be to help to alleviate it. One may select some of these responses and choose to call them alone 'moral', for example, helping other people. On the other hand, it may be better to take morality in a very wide sense, thinking of it as the sort of response which all sorts of apprehended realities demand, when rightly apprehended. Learning to be moral would then be learning how to respond appropriately and sensitively to the many situations of human experience, and that would include the appreciation of music as well as care for the sick and lonely.

One may feel inclined to say that musical appreciation is not a moral matter. The reason for that is probably that some people cannot appreciate music; that we think of it as a leisure-activity rather than a duty; and that it hardly seems able to compete with, say, the claim to save a drowning child. These things are so. Some people are not musical, but to lack any artistic appreciation at all is to lack a human excellence, and to pursue such appreciation as one can is a virtue. The degree of obligation depends upon ability, opportunity, and alternative possibilities; but I am quite prepared to say that if you can appreciate art, and do not do so, and do not practice any other comparable activity, you are failing in your duty as a person; your are failing to respond appropriately to features of your human situation. The fact that such appreciation is pleasant is irrelevant; indeed, we have a duty to cultivate a rich leisure-life, if we are able.

The real difficulty comes when one compares concert-going with sick-visiting. Of course the latter is in general

more important, for sick people have real and definite
needs, whereas music simply offers us a human enrichment.
There is no question that saving a dying child takes
precedence over going to a concert. Yet that does not mean
that concert-going is not a duty at all. If we think about it,
there are always so many people in dire need that we could
spend all our time in catering for those needs and doing
nothing else. But we do not do so; we still spend part of
our time in leisure pursuits. In other words, we do not
always put the needs of others before cultural aims. We
try to achieve a balance between self-realization and helping
others; and that means that the needs of others do not
always, in every situation, over-ride cultural aims. So
artistic appreciation is a duty, though not a very stringent
one.

I am suggesting that one thinks of duty not as obeying
laws of conduct, which are usually unpleasant, nor as
following principles that one just makes up; but as learning
to make appropriate responses to the various factors in our
experience and to achieve an adequate view of those factors,
a right balance between them, and an increasing sensitivity
to their nature. We do not have to intuit moral properties
or propositions, mysteriously dangling in the universe; we
simply have to see and respond to all the realities we daily
encounter. In some ways, this view is nearer emotivism than
to prescriptivism; for emotions are responses of the person
to features of his environment. But I am also stressing the
cognitive element in such response; we have to seek to know
more fully what is there and to direct our feelings in accordance with such growing apprehension.

The cultivation of this sensitivity, this capacity for
adequate appreciation, is distinctive of human personality.
Animals react to stimuli, and no doubt have some form of
knowledge. But they have not the capacity for appreciating
the objects of their experience for their own sake, for the
interiorization of reality through contemplation. Such an
activity requires the work of reason, penetrating to the
nature of things, and relating successive apprehensions in
time to form apprehended unities; it requires a rich and

controlled affective life and an act of will, to turn from partiality and self-concern and open oneself to what is outside oneself, to see the objective dispassionately, rather than from the point of view of what it can do for one. One may fail to realize such an attitude by not noticing what is before one; by not attending to it; by not being open and sensitive; by not relating what is there to other situations, or by failing to see its causes and consequences; and by not overcoming partiality which seeks always to use objects for one's own ends. But to cultivate that attitude is the true ground of the moral life. For it will lead to seeking an appropriate response in action to what is apprehended.

To say that one ought to adopt such a general attitude of sensitivity does say something of great significance for the way one orders one's daily life. It recommends the contemplative attitude as one to be adopted at all practicable times in one's life, but it says nothing about what is apprehended or about how to respond to it. It is notorious that people offer differing accounts of what there is to be apprehended in the world. They dispute about the nature of the world and the appropriate response to it: here insight and evaluation are inseparably connected with the cognitive quest. So one gets different understandings of the nature of man and of how one should interact with others. For this reason, one cannot be content simply to say, 'Be sensitive', for that in itself does not guarantee just perception and adequate response. The objectivist believes that some perceptions are more accurate than others and that some responses are more appropriate than others. That is why he can speak of learning, being right or wrong, and having more or less understanding. Being sensitive is certainly the way to arrive at a correct moral perception; but since people are more or less sensitive in many different ways, to adopt that method does not guarantee correctness.

The moral quest is not one of finding self-evident moral truths or intuiting particular moral commands, as though one had a special moral sense which could infallibly put one in touch with true propositions. It is a matter of seeking a more adequate understanding of human beings—and

27

indeed of all beings—and of finding the apt response to such being. The questions, 'What is being?' and 'How am I to respond to being?' are the fundamental moral questions; and to achieve a full insight into the nature of being and to respond in a way fully adequate to our own personality, is to see what is true in morality. This quest is no way to infallibility; it is fraught with risk and hesitancy, inevitably conditioned by our own presuppositions and interests; and it is a quest on which we need often to be guided by others who have a more adequate perception of reality than we do, or a more sensitive capacity for response to it. But it is a quest which each of us must finally undertake for ourselves.

How will this affect the content of specific moral rules? Only in an indirect way. Our sensitivity to the world in general builds up in us a general set of responses which we consider appropriate; and this determines the way we tend to understand new situations. Then our sensitivity to particular cases seeks an understanding of all the factors involved in a certain type of case. A moral rule is usually a general principle which is a sort of shorthand guide to the kind of response we consider appropriate to a certain type of human situation. Consider, for example, the clear moral rule, 'Do not kill'. We do not intuit this as some sort of self-evident truth nor do we receive specific orders not to kill whenever we are tempted to do so. For most of us, the rule forbids a particularly extreme case of harming others; and the more subtle principle which underlies it is that one should not destroy or diminish the personal growth of another person. Thus Jesus extends the prohibition to anger, abuse, and sneering (see Matt. 5.22). For all those things tend to hurt or diminish others. They clearly express the refusal or inability to appreciate another person; anger prevents a clear view; abuse and sneering show a lack of understanding and appreciation. Sensitivity to others requires that we try to preserve and help the efforts of others to grow in personal being. We might say that not only are anger, abuse, and sneering prohibited; but, more positively, loving acceptance, encouragement, and appreciation are enjoined. We should try to understand their motives and needs, encourage them in pursuing their purposes and share in appreciating their efforts and successes. We should attempt to build up their capacity to appreciate, their abilities to create, and their capacities for mutually enhancing and accepting relationships. The centre of personal being is the capacity fully to appreciate and creatively to act in relationship with others. We realize our own person-hood, therefore, precisely in being sensitive to others and joining with them in the pursuit of their purposes.

Complications arise, of course, when persons exercise their freedom in ways which destroy themselves or their fellows; when they limit their sensitivity, act to achieve power over others, and destroy community by disruptive behaviour. Then one's own response to them needs to be modified and the all too obvious dilemmas of morality and personal relationship arise. There may then be a place for anger, opposition, and restraint of others, and it is very difficult to decide just what that place is. But the basic principle is clear, that one should help others to flourish as persons without qualification, in so far as their acts do not, in turn, harm others. The rule, 'Do not kill', is a sort of minimal expression of that principle, the prohibition of the case which is the extreme opposition to the principle. Now that principle is itself a filling-out of the principle of sensitivity, given that persons are distinguished by being free, creative, sensitive, and social beings, and that the appropriate response to them is to preserve and enhance those characteristics. It is our sensitivity which will disclose what persons are and what this positive response to their being should be; and this will happen as we build up our experience of persons and interact with them in the course of our lives, and as we talk with those who may be more perceptive or sensitive than ourselves.

The Christian who sees morality as rooted in objective reality will see the moral life as a growth in sensitive response to all those situations which he meets in his experience. He will also claim that behind and sustaining all the finite realities that he apprehends is the presence of God;

and because of that fact, he will naturally tend to interpret his experiences in terms of relationship to God, in biblical language, in terms of situations of gift, demand and judgement. Not always, but at certain times, unpredictably and uncontrollably, God may grant some special grace, giving the gift of inner peace, joy, and a sense of his overflowing power. He may come to us in judgement, making us aware of some failing in our lives which needs to be checked, or he may demand from us some course of action, such as being ordained or tithing our income. The man who tries to be sensitive to the being of God at all times is liable to have many experiences of this sort; but they are characterized by being uniquely personal and unpredictable; they are, as we say, 'of grace'. The Christian's sensitivity will naturally be radically affected by the fact that it is primarily and always open to God as well as towards people, works of art, and so on. But the Christian's relation to God is fundamentally the same as his relation to all beings; it is a seeking for fuller and deeper knowledge and appreciation of being and for the response in action and attitude which is appropriate to it. The morality of the Christian is a morality of response.

5

The Divine Call

The view of morality outlined here is fundamentally different from any view which founds it simply on human inclinations and their fulfilment; and to this extent the traditional Thomist account of morality in terms of fulfilling one's natural inclinations is apt to be misleading. But one must remember that, on the Thomist account, the inclinations are implanted by God, and their true fulfilment can only lie in their orientation towards God. Moreover, the basic question of Thomistic Natural Law theorists is, like the one I have proposed, 'What is human nature, or the nature of human being?' All I am warning against is the danger of so interpreting talk of natural human inclinations that the basic question becomes, 'What do I want?' rather than, 'What does being demand of me by way of response?'

Morality is not just a question of acting so as to fulfil my own long-term desires or even the long-term desires of the greatest number of people. Human desires are not irrelevant to morality, and to respond to persons appropriately one must know what they are, which includes knowing what their desires are. Apt response to persons does not consist simply in fulfilling their actual desires, whatever they are, but in bringing them to fulfilment as persons; and the notion of fulfilment introduces the notion of an ideal, of what a person ought to be.

Rousseau said, 'Man has been born free but everywhere he is in chains'. If one starts from the actual condition of men, one may only rarely find them to be free, creative, sensitive, and sociable. At best, one can say that men have these capacities or possibilities, which distinguish them from most of the animal world, but in fact their lives may be charac-

31

terized by oppression, monotony, harshness, and competition. That is why the liberal virtues of creativity, culture, and co-operation often seem hopelessly impractical in a world where violence, oppression, and injustice infect all social structures, and why the Reformers sometimes discarded Natural Law theory, on the ground that man's natural wants and inclinations were so perverted by sin that they were no reliable guide to conduct. One may very well come to think, as Hobbes and Machiavelli did in greater or less degree, that human nature is in fact distinguished by its lust for power, accumulation of wealth, and personal pleasure, rather than by creativity, culture, and co-operation.

So there is a tension within Christian thought between regarding man as, on the one hand, made in God's image and on the other as a 'fallen' and depraved creature. Theorists who take the former view tend to look for what is distinctively human and hold that such things must be furthered, whereas those who take the latter view tend to regard actual human nature as under judgement, preserved only by divine forbearance, condemned by the absolute moral law of God, to be accepted only under grace and by faith. It is, however, possible to combine something of both these views and thus achieve a balanced Christian perspective on human nature. The latter, Protestant-Augustinian view, preserves the absoluteness of the divine command—'You shall do this'—in face of human attempts to compromise or find a reasonable adjustment to one's inclinations. It keeps man as he is open to God's judgement, and removes all complacency at the thought of successfully living out a humane and reasonable ethical code. But it also may tend to make morality irrational; the sheer assertion of absolute duty, commanded without reason or further justification, may lead to an unthinking obedience and a rejection of reason as a guide to action at all.

On the other hand, a study of human nature, its needs and capacities, preserves the Christian belief that God created man 'in his own image', for freedom, creativity, and love, which are the characteristics of the divine being. Man is a purposive being, and his capacities are God-given, so that morality is not irrational; its rational basis is the pursuit of those human characteristics which bring creation to its proper end and fulfilment; but such a view can lead, and historically sometimes has led, to a comfortable acceptance of human nature as it is, and the replacement of the driving ideal and call of duty by the reasonable accommodation to one's desires and needs. It has even led to the sub-personal view that the purposes of nature as such are not to be impeded; so that human freedom is restricted by the given conditions of his biological nature. If there is to be a Natural Law, it must be founded on the value and the ideal of personality, not on certain biological contingencies of evolution.

What is needed, then, is a view which combines the absolute moral demand which is enshrined in the Torah, with the acceptance of a divine purpose in the creation of persons, which means that God's will cannot contradict our human nature, as he intended it in creation, but must fulfil it ultimately by uniting it to himself in love. One must look at human nature, then, not only to see what it actually is, but to see what the divine purpose, the fulfilment of that nature must be. The Christian response is not just to man, but to the claim of God revealed in and through his creatures to bring them to fulfilment.

But how can one discern this claim in everyday moral experience? How does the divine command come to be known? The situation is very complicated, because the assertion of God's existence is not an assertion of fact from which evaluative conclusions can be derived. It is itself an evaluation of existence: that being is grounded in meaning and value which is personal and holy. One's interpretation of morality may itself be one of the grounds of a cumulative argument for theism, rather than just a derivation from it. The matter is one of finding a coherent set of ways of dealing with one's life, rather than of marshalling a deductive set of principles, beginning with the clearest or simplest. We begin with our own complex situations, and work from there, finding how various beliefs and evaluations slot into

33

each other, or fail to do so, as we work towards a never attained integrated understanding of the world, which enables us to live appropriately in it.

So one may find God in the world, as the demand implicit in certain realities to preserve or perfect them; in another's need or our own aspiration to fuller life. One should not think of a set of moral principles, waiting to be inspected, or of a set of properties of trees and tables to be seen by a mysterious moral sense. But we are able to see the possibilities of beings; and as they more nearly approach the personal, so we can see more possibilities with greater diversity, complexity, and adaptability. We say that we see what a certain person could be; that a child 'has it in him' to be a great poet; that someone needs care and attention. Moreover, in our own case we see how we could be more sensitive, sympathetic, or reverent; and so we can generalize to imagine other persons as centres of moral effort to be sensitive to each other in a harmonious community. We come to see, more or less well, depending on our insight, rational dispassionateness and critical judgement, how human reality could be and ought to be, what fulfils and what diminishes. The demand to seek what fulfils may break in upon us in many ways—there is no one formula—but it is always the voice of God, the call of a holy, morally demanding reality. It may come in a moment of seeing suddenly someone's need, in reflecting on the facts of human life, in prayer, or it may emerge gradually, without being noticed, in the practical activity of relating with other persons and learning to grow together. We may never think of it or it may shatter us in a moment of insight by showing us that others are people who claim our attention. Whether it is mediated through finite creatures, comes in a sudden insight, or slowly forms as a conviction in the course of our thinking, the call of being is to be open and sensitive to others, and co-operate in bringing them to perfection. Since it is the demand of God made upon us it is transcendent to all finite realities, but it may be mediated through them and it is certainly particularized in them.

Why be open to other beings? Because it is demanded.

By whom? By one who is holy, who demands absolutely and categorically. The exact formula of the demand, the way in which it comes, the extent and depth which we perceive it to have, the force it has, these vary. But its ground is the same, that there God calls beings to a moral purpose with a peremptory personal address. So we may say that 'Do not take unfair advantage', is an insight which came to us when we were tempted to take Tommy's toy as a child. It did not extend to Freddy, but only to our friends, and the sense of unfairness was only concerned with playtime situations; and we did not feel it absolutely, but only as quite important. Nevertheless, here God called us personally and uniquely. In responding to such demands and building up in thought and action, and by being trained by example and precept, a general set of attitudes to types of situation, we may make the principle a more sophisticated one of justice, or equality of consideration for all; we may extend it to all men in all situations, and regard it as a basic moral principle, never to be contravened. We may live our lives in the pursuit of it, fighting oppression and injustice. But however we take it, what underlies it is the call of being to co-operate in perfecting his creatures. Being is personal, holy, purposive, and creative; these are the elements in reality which underlie this objectivist view of morality.

Christians should oppose any account of ethics which makes it less than the encounter with a holy, purposive Creator. It is not meant that we must recognize what one encounters to be God nor that we must have a series of special religious revelations, but only that we must recognize and respond to the demand in whatever situation it is disclosed to us. So we cannot ground ethics on a sense of personal injustice, coupled with sympathy for our fellows; or solely on human desires or rationality or feelings of approval or sympathy. Natural Law theory is right in stressing that the moral course is to perfect human nature, as created by God. To that we must add that we must do this in response to the objective demand to fulfil God's purpose, a non-exponible moral demand. Kant was right in seeing that Aristotelian/Thomist ethics have not stressed

6

Purpose

The third main element in the conception of duty as obedience to the will of God is that it interprets morality in terms of a personal purpose in the universe. We have already seen how the moral demand is basically to aim at the perfecting of creatures and, since personality is the supreme ground of all things, to aim specifically at the fulfilling of those qualities which are distinctive to man as person. If one lacks such a belief in the purposive ordering of the world, talk of distinctive qualities of persons becomes arbitrary; for if there is no real purpose, there are no proper or true characteristics of man as such, which he ought to fulfil. So lack of belief in purpose will undermine any view which rests morality on fulfilling distinctive qualities of person-hood.

The notion of divine purpose in the world is, of course, very complex. We cannot hold, like Aristotle, that all things act to attain their proper end, like stones falling to earth because they want to reach the centre. Final causality of that sort has been ostracized from our view of nature, and the theory of natural selection must certainly affect any theories of a divine plan in evolution; the element of random mutation and chance selection is too well established to be overthrown by a naive belief in direct divine planning of all details of evolution. Moreover, since we do accept the fact of evolution, we cannot conceive the divine purpose as a static, rather short-term thing. It must be a growing, developing, creative process of emergence.

For instance, one probably should not say that God planned that a creature just like man would emerge in the evolutionary scheme; but personal qualities of knowledge, feeling, and will were destined to emerge, in whatever specific form. The general outlines of personal growth and the goal of union with the Creator are set by the very nature of God, but much is left for creative emergence and for variety in detail, in the creation. One may thus speak of a very general purpose in creation—to achieve personal being capable of relationship to the Creator—but of great variety and room for creative ingenuity in the means of achieving this purpose. On this view, to co-operate in God's purposes is to respond to his general goal of fulfilment, but also to be creative and imaginative in the exercise of human skills and capacities, in particularizing this purpose in more specific ways. Perhaps, to use a crude analogy, one might say that God's purpose is that we should write a play with a beginning, middle, and end, but we respond to that purpose by creative ingenuity in doing the writing, by inventing unforeseen tangles in the plot, and by skill in developing a precise story. So the capacity for free and creative action is most important in the human response to the divine will. Our purpose is not laid down in precise detail, as something to which we may obediently conform; it is to be worked out by creative response to the intention of God, which draws us towards a dimly conceived goal of perfection, whose lineaments must be filled in precisely by our creative action.

Since God is the Lord of history, and not just the changeless eternal but remote Creator, there may be, and Christians believe, often are, particular purposes which God calls men to fulfil in their lives; this is what we mean by vocation to a particular task or calling. In addition to the general divine will that all men should achieve fulfilment by their creative response to his demands, there are often particular purposes which God calls men to implement. It may be that no such call will come to us, but we must remain open to the possibility of such a particular calling, a purpose which is peculiarly ours, which we are obliged to pursue. Whether or not such a sense of vocation is part of our moral experience, there is an important sense in which each of us has a unique purpose. We are not just particular cases of a general purpose of fulfilment; for the doctrine of the incarnation stresses the unique importance of the individual human life. Each of us has a unique purpose, the fulfilment of our own individual gifts and virtues, which we must pursue in our own way.

It is not possible to reduce morality without remainder to one or two very general principles like 'perfect human nature'. Each of us in our own situation is obliged to seek the fulfilment of a purpose which is uniquely our own. Again, this is not pre-ordained in complete detail; our response to the moral demand must be a creative one. Yet the demands made upon us, in their detail and complexity, give each of us a unique historical destiny and moral worth. In particular human situations which have a place in history and culture, the will of God, as it were, splits up, so that the demand is expressed in a number of disparate and often conflicting values, to which we must respond. It is important for the Christian that he not only sees one general principle of responding to the demand to perfect personality but also finds specific demands implicit in his own situation, to realize many kinds of value, and to fulfil a uniquely individual moral purpose, the will of God for his irreplaceable life. These values, of course, all come within the limiting rubric of fulfilling personality, but they are not deducible from it, simply in conjunction with factual premises. They are claims addressed to the Christian in his own situation, intimating a moral purpose for his life. So the Christian will not only see morality as a matter of general principles to be pursued or values to be realized but as the pursuit of an individual moral purpose, the fulfilment of a destiny, by creative response to a contextualized demand.

Moreover, the purpose of God is a personal one. The fulfilment of humanity is to consist in personal relationship, and the goal of life is personal relationship to God in the communion of saints, the fellowship of all believers. Man is not an isolated being, but lives in community, and so he is called to extend and deepen the sense of community, of mutual love. The Christian obligation is to be members of the Kingdom of God, a society in which love, justice, and peace can be found. There is a positive obligation on

Christians to build up a community in which human fulfilment can be found, ideally by all; and so there is a positive
conception of justice as the pursuit of a society in which men
can find their own fulfilment in co-operation with others.
Any easy solutions in this area are ruled out by the per-
vasiveness of self-interest and human greed, but the basic
obligation is clear, and founded directly on the nature of
God's creative act in calling into being creatures to relate
to him in love, that one must creatively pursue fulfilment in
co-operation, and therefore build up society to make such
creative co-operation (and creative conflict, too) possible.
This is something more than keeping the peace, to let men
pursue their private ends. It is a stress on the community
as such, as a goal of moral endeavour, though in such a way
that individual fulfilment is not diminished but extended by
mutual relationship.

A humanist may agree on all these principles, though
he will be likely to interpret 'vocation' in a subjective way,
as referring to what meets our needs or interests, but it
should be clear by now that morality is not just a question
of which principles one accepts. What really counts is how
one meets and interprets one's experience, though I do think
that the collapse of a purposive interpretation of life
altogether would result in a devaluing of personal worth.
An eminent biologist has remarked that if one sees men
as simply bundles of large molecules, one's view of them
changes radically. The Christian will regard others as
destined, in the will of God, for fulfilment, which will give
them an ultimate value in his eyes. He will see his own
action as a creative response to and co-operation with God,
which gives a strong motivation to his conduct. He will look
for a point and purpose in his own life, and see the ideal of
a society of mutual love and respect as divinely imposed
upon him. So his actual living-out of the moral life will
have a distinctive tone, as the discovery of and co-operation
with an absolutely binding purpose in the universe, and an
exploration of fuller relationship with God, the ground of
all beings, and with his fellow-men, as made in the image of
God, and destined to be conformed to his likeness. His way

of seeing, and consequently of responding to, the world, will in these ways be distinctively theistic; and will give a rational foundation to whatever moral principles he accepts and a specialized interpretation of them.

The introduction of the concept of God does provide a rationale for the moral attitude which is lacking in non-theistic views. The Christian sees God as perfect being and Creator; so the world reflects and aims to embody his perfections; all things have a possible perfection, at which they aim; so one derives the moral principle of aiming at the natural perfecting of creatures. The Christian sees God as the Judge of all men; moral conduct becomes a constant choosing of life or death, enriching or diminishing one's personal being; so one derives the moral principle of aiming at moral perfection in one's own life. The Christian sees God as the redeemer of the world, working in one to make one whole, as one turns to him in faith; so one derives the moral principle of seeking liberation from the structures of the world and its standards, to find a moral goal in relationship to the Creator.

Because there is a Creator whose reality is personal, and because beings reflect his perfections in various ways, these moral injunctions to seek natural and moral perfection and freedom from constraining factors in one's personality and environment are given a wider intelligibility. They embody appropriate responses to the fact that person-hood is the highest value, and is to be perfected by co-operation in creative responsiveness. This is not an arbitrary attitude; in a theistic context it is the appropriate responsive understanding of the world as a whole. For theism, God is the purpose and inner nature of all being; he is the ontological base of all reality; and to respond to him is to respond to being's real nature.

A materialist has not got this sort of intelligible context for morality. He cannot see personal reality as the *telos* and ground of being. Persons must be parts of matter without a fundamental ontological primacy, and there can be no place in a materialist view for talk of moral demands or imperatives which 'really' exist. If only matter exists, there is no place for moral demands to be; they would be ontological oddities, without intelligible placing in the world. But the theist can add moral demands into his ontology; he can say that there are features which claim our responsive allegiance, whether we actually respond or not; there are demands which actually exist, and so are ignored at our peril. These demands are intelligibly grounded in the will of a knowing, personal creator who sets the goal of beings, and draws them towards it by his demands, sustenance and promises. In this sense, theism provides the ontological foundation which makes a morality of concern for personal worth both intelligible and appropriate, as a response to the nature of reality.

7

Man's Final End

We are now in a position to attempt a general interpretation of Christian morality in outline, and to suggest how the will of God gives rise to specific human duties. It has been suggested that the basic theistic principle is to co-operate in bringing creatures to fulfilment and, in particular, to sustain and further distinctively personal qualities, to realize distinctive human qualities both in oneself and in others. To work this out in more detail, we need to consider what those basic human qualities are, the furtherance of which fulfils our distinctive nature, which enables us to fare well, to achieve *eudaimonia*, in Aristotle's term, which is often misleadingly translated as 'happiness'. This is itself an evaluative task, for it involves picking out some qualities as especially important, as fulfilments of personality. Aristotle himself chose contemplation as the most characteristic personal activity; a term which Aquinas transmuted into *beatitude* or blessedness, the vision of God which completely satisfies all human desire. We may think that rather too static and theoretical a virtue, and there is certainly a tension between such rational contemplation and the resurrection of the body, which may seem to be rather a superfluous appendage for one whose end is the simple attention to God.

We may be more disposed to think of creative activity, which is in some sense embodied in a common world of concerns and activities, as more essential to the continuance of what we value in human personality. Nevertheless, it is clearly true that the capacity to know, understand, and appreciate is a distinctive human excellence; in man it goes far beyond what exists in the rest of the animal world. In the understanding of nature through scientific exploration; the appreciation of beauty in art and the world, in imaginative empathy with other persons, and in the contemplative quest of religion the person is able to savour, explore, and delight in the appreciation of the nature of the environment in which he has his being and in openness to it. One distinctive human capacity is this sensitivity or openness to values outside oneself. It is thus a duty to realize this capacity in oneself, by cultivating such sensitivity in as many ways as possible, and to help others to realize it by providing the training and conditions for its exercise, and co-operating in activities which enhance it. The ways in which we do this and the extent to which we do it naturally will depend on our circumstances and other claims upon us. One might say that sensitivity is an asymptotic ideal, which we never fully attain, but which always draws us on to further efforts; it is the ideal or value of knowledge in its widest sense.

Associated with the value of knowledge, yet distinct from it, is the value of rationality. If knowledge is concerned more with the achievement of a state of contemplation or cognition, rationality is concerned with the way one makes practical decisions; it is what has traditionally been called prudence. Man must use reason to work out laboriously and hesitantly what he must do, and it is his duty to cultivate his capacity to reason in order to calculate consequences dispassionately and discount partiality and prejudice. It is his duty, too, to promote the use of reason in others, by training, encouragement, and the promotion of discussion and rational argument.

A capacity which is just as central as contemplation and reason, and which may be more apparent to us in a technological age than it was in medieval times, is the capacity for free creative action, for the use of skills to create and pursue long-term goals. We value not only the ability to appreciate music, but also the ability to create music; and one might well say that appreciation is itself a repetition of creation, that there is a creativeness involved in proper appreciation already. If free creative action is a distinctive human good, then we have a duty to pursue and extend our own creative capacities in all sorts of fields, in work, art, play, or personal relations. We have also a duty to preserve and extend the freedom of others, to train them in skills and maintain the conditions for their exercise, and to co-operate with them in the pursuit of their creative purposes.

Another distinctive personal good is the social relationships in which man is involved. To be a person, in the full sense, is to interact with and relate to other persons, and we become the persons we are because of the relations we develop with others. There is thus an inescapably social dimension to human fulfilment, which gives rise to a duty to pursue many types of social relationship ourselves and to create a society in which such relationships may grow and flourish, a harmonious system of co-operative purposes, within which personal creative freedom is not diminished but extended by faithful contact with others.

One has here, then, an outline of the duties which are involved in seeking human fulfilment. With regard to ourselves, we shall pursue sensitive appreciation of nature, persons, art, and prayer; we shall pursue dispassionate rationality in decision-making; we shall seek to realize our capacity for many creative purposes, to extend our personal relationships by friendship with others. With regard to others, we shall seek to cherish them as persons, for their individuality, to extend the range of their creative actions, to co-operate in achieving their purposes, to seek friendship in shared pursuits, and to maintain a society in which mutual freedom is maximized. In this pursuit of common fulfilment, happiness will naturally be found. So happiness does not need to be sought as a separate goal; it naturally follows upon the successful achievement of one's rational purposes in co-operation with others. These conditions of fulfilment are formal conditions, in that they do not mention the specific goods which are sought by men but only how humanity is to be fulfilled in the pursuit of such goods. So they can be regarded as limiting principles, laying down the limits of the permissible purposes which men may pursue.

But there are two main respects in which the account may be thought deficient. First, some important characteristics of human being have been entirely omitted: the elements of our animal nature, the instincts and desires of hunger, sex, aggression, security, and limited sociability. These have been omitted because they are not distinctive of persons, but are common to animal nature. Yet persons are animals, too, and something must clearly be said about these characteristics. Secondly, the whole account has been outlined as though we lived in an ideal world in which everyone would agree in pursuing these purposes, if only they were clearly outlined. But we must consider the essential human capacity to ignore or reject the moral demand, and the consequent only-too-obvious tendency of men to oppress and degrade their fellows. The moral life, in practice, is a warfare against evil in ourselves and others, and something must be said about this if the account is to be realistic at all.

What I have done, in working out those distinctive human qualities which man is called to pursue by God, is to outline a doctrine of the *imago Dei* in man, to show those respects in which man can reflect and express in his own being the being of God and in which he reflects the image of God. If we consider the complex Christian doctrine of God as Trinity, the essential characteristic of whom is love, we must attribute to God beatitude, knowledge, wisdom, creativity, and community. For God knows his own being fully and possesses perfect happiness in the creative act of love within the Trinity, and acts with perfect wisdom to create finite beings to express his glory. If we ask in what respects man is created in God's image, then perhaps we can say that it is in his capacity to possess perfect happiness by growth in knowledge and in creative acts of love in fellowship with other persons. Ultimately, this knowledge and love is of God himself, and we express the glory of God by our creative response to the vision of his love in the community of all rational creatures. The final end of man is to grow in perfect love for God in community; such a community of persons, living in peace, joy, and love, would be the perfect image or icon of God's being, the fulfilment of his design in creating the universe. It is this final ideal of personal being which Christians find to be expressed in Jesus, and it is by the standard of such an ideal that we must measure the actual life of man in the world, and the duties which bind him to the pursuit of that ideal.

Thus man is created in the image of God, in his capacity for possessing the very life of God by a growth in knowledge, love, and personal relationship. But man is also a creature, who has come to be by an evolutionary process and in a universe where events are governed by general laws of physics and statistical probabilities governing chance mutations. In the course of evolution, the laws governing the primary physical realities have developed and become more complex, so that there has been a sort of continuing creative urge in created being to develop and change; but this creative urge has often seemed blind or groping, resulting in dead-ends and abortive experiments. Man himself is a result of random mutations and natural selection, and though theists believe that God is the general directing and creative power behind this process, it seems undeniable that the evolution of man is part of a process characterized essentially by trial and error, slow struggle, rising and falling, in which suffering and struggle are part of creaturely freedom. Man, seen in this perspective, is part of evolving, struggling nature, and the biological, psychological and social heritage of his past must be taken into account when considering how the ideal of the *imago Dei* can be realized in actual human life.

It is because most educated people now accept this view of man's place in the world that many traditional formulations of Natural Law are unacceptable. They assumed a view of the world as directly created by God without evolutionary development and as a place in which all suffering and evil were a result of Adam's historical fall from grace. We are now much more aware of how our animal instincts have evolved naturally and are an inescapable part of our nature. Thus they cannot simply be condemned, but must be used and channelled wisely to the eventual attainment of our final end. So the basic principle that we can accept is that our animal nature is entirely natural, is inescapably rooted in us as the product of a long evolutionary development, and must be accepted as such. But it must be modified and controlled as far as possible to bring into being the ideal of the Kingdom of God, the community of love, aroused by the vision of God, which is our final end, in the will of God. What must be undertaken now is an analysis of the main elements which may be assumed to constitute human nature, so that one may fill out a little the sorts of moral principle which a Christian will find implicit in his status as a creature of God, rooted in a long and developing history, and destined for a free and creative future.

8

Duties of Survival

The most basic instinct of all is that of survival. This is basic, not only in the sense that it is in fact very strong in most animals, but also in that it is a precondition of any form of fulfilment. So it is an instinct which can be readily cultivated by the Christian. The drive to survival is sometimes criticized on the ground that it is a very selfish thing, but on an evolutionary view, it is survival of the species which is important, not survival of the individual; so that it can give rise to acts of heroic self-sacrifice for the sake of other members of the species or the tribal group. Certainly, the moralist will think of survival not only as survival of one individual, but of all individuals of the same type, regarded as of approximately equal importance, except in special circumstances. But the moralist must avoid the temptation of saying that, because a thing happens, it is therefore right. Herbert Spencer held that the natural world is one in which only the fit survive and concluded that morality enjoins a policy of ruthless self-interest or the survival of the fittest. T. H. Huxley, on the other hand, in a famous essay, *Evolution and Ethics*, agreed that nature is 'red in tooth and claw', but concluded that man ought to oppose this process in the name of love and sympathy. It seems clear that, just because 'nature' acts in a certain way, it does not follow that man must, or even that he should, if he has the choice. The view being taken here is, that since human nature is a creation of God, destined for the end of union with him, an analysis of its biological, psychological, and sociological components may disclose the respects in which the divine purpose ought to be pursued, within the limits of our 'given', historically conditioned nature. One is not

49

saying that, because humans have a strong drive to the survival of the species, one ought *therefore* to implement that drive. One is saying that the existence of such a drive may well be a limiting factor on the sorts of conduct that it is reasonable to expect of men, since it forms a certain sort of restriction on total freedom of action. It must be taken into account in any estimate of man's possible moral performance and consideration of it may suggest how it can be used and modified to realize the moral destiny of man.

Since survival is a precondition of any form of fulfilment whatsoever, and since our primary obligation is that creatures should be brought to their proper fulfilment, one can say that there is a positive obligation to do all one can to increase peace and security and the conditions of human survival in general, such maximization of the conditions of survival is positively enjoined. Conversely, it is prohibited, or morally forbidden, to take life or injure oneself or others. One sees here how duties fall into four main types. The first two are the positive duties to oneself and to others: these are the things which are morally enjoined on one to do and they are usually not very specific on how much should be done, or how often, or at what time. To take the example with which we are now dealing, one must take some action to increase security in society—perhaps by starting 'good neighbour' schemes, or joining a racial harmony group—but the exact action is not specified, or how much time one should spend doing it, relative to other things, or how much it is reasonable to do. These are things which must be worked out by the individual himself, matters of judgement and personal evaluation of priorities. The principle itself does not specify these matters, and it would be silly to suppose that there is an exact quantifiable answer to such questions. One can say that it is possible to do too much, to the neglect of other things or that it is possible to do too little, by neglect or oversight, but there is a great deal of latitude in the middle as to exactly what should be done. The last two types of duty are negative duties to oneself and to others: the things which are morally prohibited. They are

usually quite specific, in our present case, the prohibition
of suicide and murder, for example; cases which leave no
latitude as to what should be done, when or how, or to what
extent. One can see here, too, the difference between stating
what an instinct or basic drive is and using it as a basis for
a moral judgement. For it seems true that not all men want
to survive, or there would be no suicides. But that is not the
point; the point is that man ought to survive, as a condition
of pursuing that human fulfilment to which one is obligated
by God. Survival is very important as a condition of any
fulfilment but, on the other hand, it is not intrinsically
important, for its own sake; mere survival is not particularly
valuable.

There are four main human drives involved in the general
drive to survival: hunger, sex, aggression, and tribal loyalty.
To survive one must eat, and therefore one must hunt,
cultivate or procure food in some way. But whereas one can
talk of fulfilling and extending one's knowledge or creative
abilities, it is odd to talk of fulfilling or extending one's eating abilities. One may have a positive duty to increase the
food-supply and feed the hungry and a negative duty to
refrain from starving oneself or others, but eating clearly
seems not to be an intrinsic good, though it may be very
pleasant. Eating is important as a means to survival and, in
some cultures, as an aid to conviviality and social life, but
to eat well, to be a gourmet, is not a human ideal to be
achieved even at the cost of effort and struggle. It is not in
itself morally wrong to delight in good food and wine but
neither is it morally right. It is a permissible pleasure which,
like all other permissible pleasures, must be controlled by a
vision of the higher ends of humanity, the development in
ourselves of the *imago Dei*, the human fulfilment to which
God, the ideal of personal being, calls us.

To survive as a species, sexual reproduction must take
place. By analogy with food, this seems to give rise to a
positive duty to propagate the species and care for children
and a negative duty not to undermine social institutions
which regulate the procreation and nurture of children.
Regarded as a mechanism of species-survival, sex is only

important as a means to the procreation of children. It must therefore be subordinated to the demands of the procreation and care of children. But the sexual instinct is extremely strong and cannot be considered solely in that light. Sexual intercourse cannot be considered as a moral duty in itself. It is only a general duty to procreate and, even then, it is limited by considerations of more general human welfare, such as the 'population explosion', of which we are so much aware today. But intercourse is both pleasant in itself and is used to express personal love in a particularly intense way. It may thus be viewed as a permissible pleasure and as a means of expressing one intense form of human relationship in love. As such, it must always be controlled by the higher duty of personal fulfilment in community and must be restrained at those points at which it impedes or hinders such fulfilment, or even threatens to degrade and diminish human personality. Apart from that, the positive duties to do with the sexual instinct are really concerned with the care of children, that children should have an adequate and loving upbringing and early training. Negative sexual prohibitions, which seem to loom so large in human morality, are primarily concerned with preserving the conditions of child-care from disorder and insecurity.

To survive as a species, man has had to be aggressive, to preserve his group or species from attack and to establish dominion over other species which compete for available resources. Aggression, like sex, is a strong and ineradicable part of man's evolutionary heritage, which has played an essential part in his coming to a position of prominence on earth. But aggression becomes counter-adaptive in a situation like ours, when we possess weapons capable of destroying the whole world, and when nations war against each other because of envy, greed, or fear. One can derive the duties corresponding to the instinct of aggression by considering the rightful function óf aggression in the struggle for survival. This it seems, is to achieve security of existence and the rational control of the available resources for continued existence as a species. So one derives the positive duty of seeking peace, security, and order and of using available natural resources for the greatest well-being of all (the duty of distributive justice). One also derives the negative duty of not undermining social order and not misusing natural resources or distributing them unfairly.

Unlike eating and sexual intercourse, being aggressive is not in itself a permissible pleasure nor does it normally express human friendship or conviviality. Nor is it an intrinsic good. It is a strong instinct which has been necessary to human survival, and which cannot be simply eradicated now. The greatest problem the Christian faces with aggression is therefore how he can use it at all to contribute to human fulfilment. It clearly must be sublimated to subserve creative purposes; and this may be done by providing opportunities for competitive sports or in business or by creative pursuit of adventure and effort in different cultural spheres. There are many ways in which aggression can be channelled and sublimated, and a rational society will take care to provide such socially acceptable ways, which do not harm or destroy others. An important corollary of this is that the recognition of the existence of aggression, and the consequent provision of means for its sublimation, by the provision of competitive enterprises, must be part of a rational morality. So the existence of aggression gives rise to a secondary duty to find positive ways of using aggression in socially constructive ways, and a duty not to use aggression to hurt or harm others.

To survive as a species, mankind developed a natural but limited sociability, a sort of tribal loyalty which could give adequate defence in a hostile world and provide the necessary means for survival, by specialization of function within the tribe. So loyalty and altruism are deeply rooted in human nature but they have rather narrow limits, being confined to a relatively small tribal group. They are not naturally extendable to outsiders, let alone to all mankind. With this characteristic, one is moving into a more distinctively human area, for sociability is bound up with culture and language, which are distinctively personal phenomena. One may be said to have a positive duty to strengthen and extend one's natural sympathy and fraternal feeling for one's family or comrades, and to take a special care for members of one's own group; and there is a negative duty not to betray or neglect one's own tribe or family.

At this point, moral difficulties arise. For, while such limited loyalty is a strong element in human nature in general, it is also the source of one of the major obstacles to achieving a world-wide community in which purposes can be co-operatively and freely pursued. It divides men into 'insiders' and 'outsiders', and readily gives rise to inter-group conflict and suspicion. Here is the genesis of one of those genuine moral conflicts which characterize human life. The conflict is between the maintenance of one's own culture and the development of a wider society in which conflict can be overcome by mutual acceptance. It is the problem of one's duty to one's country or national interest, and one's duty to the brotherhood of man or international co-operation. But, though this often appears as a genuine problem, it seems quite clear that tribal loyalty, like the other natural instincts of man, is to be implemented and pursued only so far as it does not impede human fulfilment in general. To deepen and extend one's family, group and national loyalties and responsibilities is a duty and part of human fulfilment, human nature being what it is. But this duty must always be limited and controlled by the wider duties of seeking universal human fulfilment. Wherever tribal loyalty threatens to diminish or degrade any 'outside' human being—or, indeed, to stunt the perception and sensitivity of any 'insider'—it must be eschewed, or at least modified to prevent such diminishment. And one must also seek positively to use the sense of tribal loyalty to enrich, wherever possible, the lives of others—by using the family, for instance, as a base for helping others, and not as a cosy and inward-looking exclusive group. The duties of tribal loyalty, while real, are relatively low-level duties (rather like the duties of one's role or 'station'). They must be punctiliously performed and taken seriously. But they must also be constantly measured against the wider moral considerations of the good that is being done to men in general by their existence and pursuit. And, in cases of real conflict, the duties of tribal loyalty must always give way to the duties of general human benevolence.

These are the general principles of duty which can be derived by a consideration of man's biological nature, seen in the light of a primary obligation to fulfil human nature and realise the *imago Dei* fully in man. They have yet to be supplemented by consideration of other aspects of human nature, and so the account is at no point self-sufficient, and nothing that has been said should be taken as final and complete. Nevertheless, it is salutary to consider one thing at a time, and a systematic consideration of the general principles of morality can only increase the clarity and judiciousness which one can later bring to bear on the resolution of particular moral problems. With this in mind, we can now move on from considering the purely biological aspects of human nature, to those psychological aspects which probably seem more important and more obviously human to most people.

9

Duties of Pleasure

Man is not only an animal which strives for survival; he is also a sentient being which seeks for pleasure. Men are naturally moved to action by many sorts of consideration; but it is always a good reason for doing something that one wants to do it, that one finds pleasure in doing it. It would be an entirely unrealistic morality which attempted to ignore men's needs and desires, however complex or irrational they may seem.

All the biological factors so far mentioned—hunger, sex, aggression or the drive for power, and sociability—are natural objects of pleasure as well as being conducive to survival. But, in addition to these fairly universal bodily pleasures, there are a great number of more idiosyncratic and often sophisticated states and activities which men enjoy, from the pleasure in music to gardening, power, stamp-collecting, and lying in the sun. The things that men want and take pleasure in differ enormously from one person to another, depending upon temperament, upbringing, and inclination. So there is not much point in trying to make a list of the sorts of things men want; though no doubt, if one did, one would find that pleasure was connected with the biological needs of survival or with the uninhibited exercise of one's capacities. One can say, in general, however, that the pursuit of pleasure is both a rational and acceptable goal of human activity. Some thinkers have gone so far as to say that it is in fact the only rational end and must therefore be the foundation of morality. In opposition to such a view, Kant held that, though one has a duty to aim at the happiness of others by helping and not frustrating their legitimate pursuits, one has no duty to pursue one's own happiness. This, however, was because he thought that all men would do that in any case and would therefore not need to be enjoined to do so.

I do not think a Christian should take either view as it stands. Happiness must be part of God's will for man; he could not be conceived as willing misery or pain for its own sake. So it is a legitimate pursuit. One can go further, and say that it is a duty to enjoy the good things that God has made; so one does have a positive duty to pursue pleasure for oneself and others and a negative duty to refrain from inhibiting pleasure or causing pain. There are, after all, those who do not pursue their own happiness seriously enough; and accidie, or boredom and lassitude, is a sin which consists precisely in the failure to pursue happiness.

However, the duty of pursuing happiness needs to be qualified in four ways. First, it is not necessarily momentary and intense pleasure that one must pursue. For one needs to consider one's greatest happiness in the long run. If a great pleasure now—like drug-taking—will lead to misery later, it must be renounced, and often the thought of future happiness requires many present sacrifices, as when one saves for one's old age. So the rational pursuit of happiness will not be the mad pursuit of every passing whim, but the prudent calculation of what sorts of pursuits are going to be most satisfying, on the whole and in the long run; and for a Christian, the 'long run' includes the thought of eternal life, so that his actions must be those which are most con-ducive to the attainment of eternal life: those, in other words, which tend to unite him more closely to God in love. One must beware, however, of thinking that this is a merely prudential consideration; for, in fact, even belief in God and eternal life are based upon an evaluation of the world which gives the notion of moral perfection a central place in it. Though God wills the attainment of happiness, he does not just will happiness without conditions. As Kant says, he could then have created a universe of deliriously happy but thoughtless animals. God wills the attainment of hap-piness by means of a slow development and growth in personal relationships, in self-awareness, and in knowledge and understanding. Happiness is not an end-in-itself; it is the natural consequence of the fulfilment of one's end as man.

This leads to the second qualification of the pursuit of happiness. It is a well-known and lamented fact that the pursuit of pleasure for its own sake rarely satisfies or produces lasting happiness. One pursues happiness wisely when one pursues ends which one finds intrinsically satisfying for their own sake; and in pursuing them for their own sake, pleasure naturally ensues. Happiness is an extremely elusive commodity; and one cannot tell anyone how to find it by simply saying, 'Pursue it'. What one has to do is to discover activities which one thinks worth pursuing and hope that happiness will come in their pursuit. To achieve happiness, one needs to establish a pattern of life which contains a reasonable mixture of things one finds worth doing. There is an enormous variety of things that people find worth doing; the only point I am making is that we can only satisfactorily pursue pleasure by pursuing activities we take to be worthwhile. This, if you like, is a practical maxim for the pursuit of pleasure. But for the Christian, it entails that happiness can only really come when one pursues ends which are intrinsically worthwhile. These are precisely the ends of personal growth and relationship which God wills in creation. So the Christian's pursuit of pleasure is not just a calculation of long-term self-interest (though it is not opposed to that), but a pursuit of ends which are intrinsically worthwhile.

Consideration of these ends leads to a third qualification on the pursuit of happiness. All pleasures are not of equal worth, and they have sometimes been ranked (by J. S. Mill, for example) into higher (or mental) pleasures, and lower (or bodily) pleasures. Mill's argument for this division, like Aristotle's, is the notoriously bad one that people who have tried both types of pleasure will prefer one type to the other. But it is surely true that, taken simply as pleasures, there is no qualitative distinction to be found; only considerations of intensity, duration, and so on, which the Utilitarians adduce. For the Christian, the pursuit of pleasure, though it is a legitimate end and even a duty, must always be limited by considerations of human fulfilment, the pursuit of the ends set by the *imago Dei* as the goal of human action. The higher pleasures will be those which are most conducive to fulfilment: the pleasures of knowledge, culture, friendship, and rational action. The lower pleasures will be those which do not in themselves fulfil humanity: the desire for money, possessions, food, and sex. All pleasures are legitimate, unless they actually diminish and degrade humanity, but some types of pleasure are more conducive to the attainment of man's positive end than others. Therefore the rational pursuit of pleasure will aim at establishing a pattern of life which contains many types of pleasurable activity, but aims chiefly to cultivate those types of pleasure which are found in the realization of distinctively personal qualities. One may find pleasure in the pursuit of many ends, and it is right to do so. A life which consisted in nothing but the pursuit of virtue at all times would be unduly fanatical. But the pursuit of pleasurable ends must never diminish the personal fulfilment of oneself or others, and it must be directed in general and for the most part towards the higher pleasures of self-realization.

The fourth qualification which needs to be made to the pursuit of pleasure is a necessary modification of the ideal of self-realization. It can be stated in terms of the principle of equality: that no man's fulfilment is to be regarded as more important in itself than any other man's. This principle is founded on the insight that God created all men for fulfilment, not just a few. It does not mean or imply that God created all men to attain the same sort of fulfilment, in the same way or to the same degree. It is quite compatible with the existence of great human inequalities of character and ability. What it states is that all rational creatures are to be regarded as objects of God's creative and redemptive love, however this is worked out in detail. So we cannot pursue pleasures which impede the fulfilment of others and we should positively aim at pleasures which may help to bring others to fulfilment, as is appropriate for them in their situation. This may be by involving them in some co-operative creative enterprise, by training them to greater insight or sensitivity, or simply by friendship and encouragement. Again, then, we have an independent criterion for dividing pleasures into higher, lower, and prohibited. In this respect, the higher pleasures are those which build up the co-operative pursuit of purposes in society and enlarge human freedom and co-operation. The lower pleasures are those which are solely or primarily concerned with self-realization but do not harm others; and the prohibited pleasures are those which impede those activities of others which are either themselves co-operative or are not in turn harmful to others.

These criteria are rather difficult to apply in practice. We have to work out with some difficulty what sort of social pleasures are practicable and reasonable in our own situation; how we are to achieve self-realization, given our own talents and temperament; what sort of balance to achieve between both of these and the pursuit of the 'lower' pleasures; how far we may need to frustrate the purposes of others, despite the *prima facie* prohibition on doing so, to achieve some form of self-fulfilment; and whether we are ever justified in interfering with the permissible pleasures of others for their own good (for the sake of their final fulfilment). Add to this the difficulty of seeing what is really in our long-term interests, what pursuits really will bring happiness, and how conflicts between incompatible desires are to be resolved, both in ourselves and others, and even the legitimate pursuit of pleasure begins to take on a complexity too great for the time and effort needed to work it out rationally.

So morality, even as so far considered, is not a matter of automatically applying rules to cases, much less of intuiting by some direct insight what is to be done in a particular case. General principles are derived from a consideration of human nature, given the primary moral obligation to fulfil that nature. But judgement, wisdom, and reasoning are involved in measuring these principles against each other and incorporating them into an overall pattern of life. Much remains to be done, in terms of judgement and sensitivity, even when all moral principles are known. Moral decision-making is a skill, at which some people are naturally better than others; and the lives of most people, who have not the time, inclination, or ability to practise this skill to any great extent, will consequently be lived in accordance with social conventions, received maxims, and cultural determinations of behaviour which will be followed unless they seem to contradict first principles of morality in an unmistakable way. The ways and means of pleasure-seeking will be laid down in particular cultures by acceptable patterns of activity promoting specific patterns of life. These may vary from culture to culture; for there are many variant ways of promoting a rational pattern of desire-fulfilments within a social structure. Again, the principles of morality are limiting principles, laying down the acceptable limits of such diversity and the general goals of human activity. Systems of social convention for systematizing the inter-relation of conflicting desires and interests are necessary to give people guide-lines for daily conduct. But they may vary in many ways; what one must continually watch for is that they do not contradict moral principles, and that they do not detract from the capacity to achieve human fulfilment; that is, that conventions do not contravene the limits and goals of morality. Even that will not usually be an unambiguous matter; and there will be disputes as to whether a certain practice or institution does contravene morality. But that is only to be expected; for human morality must both be a matter of judgement and insight, and lay down general criteria according to which such judgement can be exercised. Any account of morality which does not contain both these elements fails to be adequate to the human situation.

10

Duties of Justice

Man has been considered as a biological and psycholgical entity, as a being who seeks for survival and pleasure; but it may well be said that man becomes a person, as opposed to an animal, when he enters into social relationships with his fellows, and that his personality is largely constituted by the set of these relationships. Culture, the creation of ways of life which can embody the social and civilized virtues and ideals, transforms the interpretation of the biological and psychological substrata upon which it is founded. Hunger, sex, and aggression become objects of cultural pursuit, embodied in institutions for wine-tasting, conventions of courtship and marriage, and hierarchical structures of political or economic power. The range of personal pleasures is enormously increased by cultural pursuits of craftsmanship and art, which depend on co-operation, tradition, and education for their existence. Moreover, man develops as a social animal by the creation of social institutions which give particular roles and responsibilities to individuals. The man who acts in his capacity as judge will be different from the same man in his role as father or an individual who pursues personal pleasures of reading and golf in his private life. I have spoken of the duty of culture at an individual level, as the duty of pursuing creative purposes in art and co-operative enterprises, of perfecting one's own talents and abilities (Cf. ch. 7). But there are further duties which belong specifically to man as a social animal, with a role or set of roles, in social institutions. These are the duties of politics, interpreted in a wide sense as the organization of social institutions. What underlies such duties is the principle of specialization,

whereby individuals take on specialist functions, some pro-
ducing food, some educating, some defending, some
legislating, and so on. Specialization is necessary in any
society and gives rise to the need for organization of these
various functions in some rational and efficient way. Basic
human needs for housing, clothing, and food must be met;
the tribe must be defended against its enemies; some system
of care for children, the old, and the sick must be devised;
and cultural pursuits must be made available for those who
wish to pursue them. As society grows more complex,
industry, agriculture, transport, the production of energy,
education, and health care become correspondingly more
complex and interdependent. There are no doubt many
quite different ways of organizing these things in a given
society but the basic problem in all is the same: how to
get the right sort of specialization and how to distribute
the products of such specialization most adequately.

In an ideal society, we might think that each individual
would be able to contribute to the society according to his
ability; and goods would be distributed according to need.
But we require some means of calculating needs and match-
ing abilities to available jobs and we have to cope with
situations where goods are scarce, or where needs are greater
than available resources. Here, we must remember that
society exists only for the fulfilment of its individual
members and that no man's fulfilment is ultimately more
important than anyone else's. This latter principle is quite
compatible with the belief that some are to attain fulfilment
in different ways than others; equality is not uniformity.
Some may need more goods for their fulfilment than others;
and some fulfilments may be relatively more important
than others to us (we value Beethoven more than John
Bloggs, in respect of art). But the principle reminds us that
no one's fulfilment, whatever it is, can be ignored; and it
must be positively aided, so far as we are able, compatibly
with aiming at every one else's.

It seems, in general, that negative prohibitions are more
stringent than positive duties. That is, the pursuit of a
positive duty can only in very exceptional circumstances

overrule a negative prohibition. This is because negative duties prohibit what is actually incompatible with fulfilment in some respect, whereas positive duties state how fulfilment is to be pursued. To fail to pursue a good is wrong, but it is worse to do something which actively frustrates or opposes a good. This distinction is sometimes made by speaking in terms of 'human rights'. A human right is what a man may morally expect of his fellows, what he can demand from them morally. To attack one of these rights is to frustrate the possibility of a person's fulfilment. Thus, following the outline of duties set out so far, each man has a right to life; to freedom from injury or interference; to security in his home and kin-group; to a share of a society's goods sufficient to survive. These are the minimal rights of every man. They may not be absolute, but they are conditions of his achieving any possibility of fulfilment. A man must not only be able barely to survive; he must have the possibility of achieving fulfilment to some degree, however small.

In addition to those minimal rights, there are other rights which we may be said to have against our society. There is the right to help in need or sickness; the right to education, medical care, and provision for old age; the right to a *fair* share of goods; and the right to participate in cultural pursuits. These rights do not merely demand that one is left alone in freedom. They demand positive action from others to ensure the conditions of fulfilment or aid in the pursuit of it. They express the principle of positive freedom, that each man should have the conditions of the fullest possible fulfilment, and be helped to achieve it so far as possible. This is just another way of formulating the principle of fulfilment, as applied to society. Society should be so ordered that it creates, protects, and extends the fullest range of compatible human choices.

Naturally, where a man is said to have rights against society, he also has duties to it. His duties are to support the organization of such a society in any way he can and to contribute to the production of those goods which are necessary to its existence. The government largely organizes the production and distribution of goods, and man has a duty to participate in government as well as in productive work. Men have very different types and levels of ability and only some have the organizational skills which make efficient government. In a complex society, government will have to make difficult decisions in allocating both tasks and goods, and so a new set of duties arises. The government has the duty of careful investigation and use of resources, and the people have the duty of obedience and participation in accordance with ability. Obedience is an important duty; for there will be many different ideas about how things should be done; we simply have to agree to follow the government's decision, or chaos would ensue.

In an ideal world, every man would have some distinctive ability, and would be prepared to use it for the common good. The most able would rule and they might have to require sacrifices from the people in times of hardship, war, or scarcity. But they would see that goods were distributed in accordance with need and the principle of equality, achieving the greatest amount of compatible individual fulfilment or freedom. A society could be called just in which each man worked as hard as it is reasonable to expect and each had goods appropriate to his own greatest fulfilment, compatible with the maximal fulfilments of others. It would be a duty to contribute to the community by work, though freedom to choose one's work would be maximized and unpleasant or undesirable work would be shared or compensated for as much as possible. Each man would receive what his own fulfilment required, though the minimal rights to survival could never be overruled simply for one's own fulfilment, and gross inequalities in the opportunities for fulfilment would be minimized. The job of government is to plan for the allocation of work and goods and this will require the imposition of restraints on individual freedom to some extent. Such restraints, however, should be the minimum compatible with efficient organiza-tion of resources and equalization of opportunities for fulfilment. Government has a positive role, too, however. That is, to promote the conditions of co-operative fulfilment: the pursuit of knowledge, variety of choice, training in skills and abilities, and cultural opportunities. It has a negative duty not to hinder the free pursuit of co-operative and creative enterprises.

In this way society will be ordered to make possible the realization of the fullest range of compatible human choices. If the existence of society limits one's choices by consideration of others, it is society which truly creates choice by releasing the individual from the constant necessity of procuring his own survival in a largely hostile environment. It is the duty of government to maximize compatible human choices, a task requiring sensitivity and judgement, in which there are no precise formulae to apply. It is our duty as individuals to see that government performs this function as efficiently as possible and to conform to its regulations, unless it markedly fails in its duty.

As well as government, there are other major social institutions for work, leisure, education, care of the sick and elderly and children, and religion. The principles governing these institutions can again be derived from the basic principles of fulfilment and equality. Each institution must be judged by its efficacy in making equitable fulfilment possible and in furthering it. Within each institution, we shall have certain rights and duties, which particularize our general human duties. For instance, a bank clerk must be honest, careful, and meticulous with figures and has a right to a fair wage. A member of an art club has a duty to pay dues and attend meetings and a right to see good art regularly. A teacher has a duty to teach children fairly and a right to respect and obedience. We all have a duty to care for the young, the sick, and the old and a right to such care ourselves. We have as Christians a duty to attend church and a right to the ministrations of a priest.

We may have a general duty to join some such institutions, as a particularization of our duty of self-realization. But are there principles governing the allocation of rights and duties within institutions? Many duties and rights may be matters of convention; as long as people are free to join or not, there is no objection to that. But to the extent that freedom of choice does not in practice exist, it is important that duties do not curtail personal freedom without giving a corresponding benefit in terms of fulfilment, either of ourselves or others. In general, institutional duties must be necessary either to the preservation of minimal rights to survival (and they must never curtail such rights, except to preserve similar minimal rights) or to a maximization of fulfilment, which is in principle open to every member. That is to say, there must be equality of opportunity of fulfilment, together with consideration of the sort of different fulfilments of which each member may be capable and desirous. This clause excludes uniformity; it means that each member must derive some benefit appropriate to his own capacities, with a general maximization of fulfilment, so long as that does not exclude opportunities for all.

To take a very brief example: a man may not like being a clerk. So he should be free to change his job, unless it is necessary to do it for the social good. We should have opportunities of advancement to jobs that we shall like (being manager, for instance). Our hours, tasks and pay must be adjusted so as to make compensating benefits available. Of course, a man may accept a subordinate role to enable someone else (a financial genius, perhaps) to use his talents better. Even so, some fulfilment, not the same sort, must be open to us, in which we find satisfaction (if a man simply finds satisfaction in his success, so much the better, of course).

Duties are unjust, where they constrain one against one's will, without possibility of contracting out, and where there is no maximization of a fulfilment or fulfilments which are genuinely open to all involved (by ability, inclination, and opportunity), or where there is no corresponding benefit in terms of an extension of freedom and satisfaction in some other area for the agent constrained. Correspondingly, a just society will be one in which there is maximum freedom of choice and all constraints are balanced by corresponding benefits for the agent or maximize the general opportunities for fulfilment (freedom and satisfaction). This principle is qualified by the existence of extreme situations in which survival itself is at stake. In such cases, duties without corresponding positive benefits may be imposed, if they are genuinely conditions of preserving minimal rights to survival for some members of society. In such cases, considerations of personal benefit are over-ridden by the strong duty to preserve minimum human rights.

One can now see what lies behind formulations of the first principle of natural law in terms of phrases like, 'To each his due'. The just society is one in which each man does his proper work and receives his proper reward. His proper work is that which he is best able to do or which is necessary to the preservation of minimal rights for all, or to the maximization of compatible fulfilments, provided that the agent has an equal opportunity to pursue his own distinctive fulfilment. His proper reward is the meeting of his distinctive needs and conditions for fulfilment, equally with the fulfilment of all, or which provides compensation for necessary constraints. There is involved here the principle of justice or fairness: that constraints must be balanced by benefits, that special effort merits special benefit, and that failure to do one's proper work merits corresponding decrease of the right to equal benefit. The principle of justice is a principle of 'balance' of constraints and benefits (or failures and penalties). It thus qualifies the principle of equality, which enjoins us to consider all equally. Equality must also be qualified by the consideration that men have different possible fulfilments. One person may like football and pop; another opera and chess. To aim at equality is to let both have opportunity to pursue what they want; to make such opportunities available equally. But obviously one does not provide the same opportunities for each; that would be inequality or uniformity.

It is a moral requirement arising out of man's social nature to aim at a just and equitable society, where the needs and desires of all are taken account of equally, and where constraints are balanced with benefits. Justice is concerned with the allocation of necessary inequalities in contribution to and benefits from society. In any reasonably complex society, these matters become almost impenetrably complicated, and I have only tried to sketch out the most basic principles of justice in society, which are founded on the primary Christian obligation to bring about the rule of God in society, in which all may realize in their own appropriate way the *imago Dei*. Such very abstract principles demand a close and accurate knowledge of the facts of any particular social situation before they can be translated into action; and they may be used insensitively or in an absurdly doctrinaire way. But it is of the utmost importance to grasp and clearly affirm these principles themselves, as the foundation of Christian moral thinking about society, and as a firm basis upon which to reason in greater detail about particular social policies which we are called upon to decide.

11

Duties of Faith

We have now considered man as a biological, psychological, and social animal. It remains to consider briefly his status as a spiritual being created by God to adore and enjoy him for ever. The traditional division of virtues into natural and theological is a rather strange one. Prudence, courage, temperance, and justice are rather arbitrarily chosen as natural virtues; but love, perhaps the most important virtue of all, is put with faith and hope into the theological bag. A much more coherent and intelligible pattern is presented if one examines the biblical documents to see what attitudes are demanded of man in his relation to God. Then one gets a rather more complex list of attitudes, which are, however, related to each other in a perfectly intelligible way. Theological virtues are those attitudes which God demands of man in relation to himself. In the end, the proper fulfilment of humanity, which I have construed as the foundational principle of Christian ethics, giving rise to particular duties upon consideration of human nature in its plurality and diversity (many men with many diverse abilities), is completely found only in relation to the being of God.

Throughout the New Testament one finds outlined the sort of response to God himself in which fulfilment is to be found. In Galatians 5.22 the 'harvest of the Spirit', the set of virtues which the Holy Spirit himself brings to fruition in us, is described thus: 'Love, joy, peace, patience, kindness, goodness, fidelity, gentleness, and temperance'. Again, in the famous 'Hymn to Love' of 1 Corinthians 13, we find that 'love is patient; love is kind and envies no one. Love is never boastful nor conceited nor rude; never selfish, nor quick to take offence. Love keeps no score of wrongs; does not gloat over other men's sins, but delights in the truth. There is nothing love cannot face; there is no limit to its faith, its hope and its endurance'. To this impressive list, one must add gratitude; for we are to 'give thanks every day for every thing to our God and Father' (Eph. 5.20). And one must at all times hallow and worship God, as our Lord commanded (Matt. 6.9). All these attitudes are theological virtues, because they are attitudes directed to God himself, as well as to his creatures; and because they arise as a response to the revelation of God's being within the Christian community and by the action of his Spirit within us. They can be arranged under three main headings, which express aspects of the life of prayer and faith which have always been felt to define the basic structure of the Christian's response to God. These are the general attitudes of reverence, penitence, and love; and the pattern of both private and liturgical prayer in the Church has always followed this basic structure. Reverence includes adoration, gratitude and humility, the response to the vision of the majesty and love of God as creator. Penitence includes the wisdom which brings self-knowledge and self-control, faith, hope and the joy of forgiveness, the response to the vision of the failure of man and the compassion of God. Love includes sympathy, justice, and the reconciliation of men to each other, the response to the redemptive activity of God reconciling men to each other and to himself.

So, standing within the tradition of the Christian revelation, we are called to adore the Creator, to depend solely upon his power, and to delight in his glory. These are interior attitudes; there is no particular physical manifestation of reverence, penitence, or love. But the growth into such attitudes transforms one's attitude to everything else in the world, as one comes to see all things in their relation to God. Thus these attitudes have a definite effect upon one's actions, but one cannot specifically say what that effect will be.

The consideration of these 'theological virtues' makes the point that Christian ethics is essentially attitudinal; it is concerned with the inculcation of interior attitudes. Is it a duty to be reverent, penitent, and loving? Yes; for these are the proper, appropriate responses to the being of God, and to fail to make them is a failure in humanity. These are theological virtues, because they only exist for one who believes in God; in our world, they cannot be duties for men in general. Yet it is slightly strange to talk of them as duties, even for a Christian; for they are rather responses to a disclosure of God's being than abstract principles. We cannot be obliged to have a divine revelation; that is a gift of grace. However, what one can be obliged to do is to prepare oneself for the possibility of such a disclosure by prayer and meditation. And, in so far as God does make himself known to us, we can be obliged to respond to him fully and adequately, to perfect our response to him. We cannot just set ourselves to be reverent by determination. But one can set oneself to pray and to perfect and cultivate reverence when it occurs. It is our duty, then, to seek God and to respond to his revelation, when it comes. It is also our duty to encourage others to adopt these attitudes, by teaching them about religion and helping them to develop such attitudes; and negatively, not to place any hindrance to the development of such attitudes.

Christian ethics is distinctive with regard to these theological virtues, for they are essentially the cultivation of responses to the nature of the God disclosed in the tradition centred on Jesus. They impose upon man an ideal of human perfection, which is very different from the ideals of Buddhism, humanism, or Marxism, for instance. The ideal is not just an optional extra to morally binding duties; its pursuit is a duty for all Christian: 'Be perfect, as your father in heaven is perfect' (that is, in the same way, by unlimited charity). A Christian does not merely have to avoid conflicting with some prohibited actions. This was the essence of Jesus' condemnation of the Pharisees; that they saw the Law as a set of rules governing external observances, which could be obeyed to the letter. But he extended the prohibition of murder to the prohibition of the attitude of anger; and the prohibition of adultery to a prohibition of the attitude of lust. So a Christian sees morality as the unrelenting pursuit of specific ideals, which can never be completely achieved; they govern the heart, and they always call one to further effort; they are asymptotic ideals.

This, in my view, is what underlies the perfectionism of the Sermon on the Mount of Matthew 5–7. The very radical phrasing of this moral teaching has led to many different interpretations of these reported sayings of Jesus. Some, like Tolstoy, have held that the teaching is to be taken literally; one must not swear oaths under any circumstances, and one must never resist violence, for example. Some, like Albert Schweitzer, have maintained that they were rules binding only on the understanding that the end of the world was at hand; emergency regulations in a crisis situation; and now that the world has not ended, they do not really apply at all. Some have held that the Sermon gives a picture of what life in God's Kingdom is really like, a way of life which arises out of God's gift of new life, and is hardly a system of moral rules at all; and some claim that the Sermon poses an impossible ideal, something really morally binding and yet literally impossible to fulfil, a paradoxical situation which brings home to us our need of forgiveness and God's grace, and exposes our sinfulness.

The literal, perfectionist view seems impossible to maintain as long as one means morality to apply to men in the violent, ambiguous world in which we live, where a measure of force and compromise is necessary to preserve the very conditions of social order. On the other hand, I see no need to leap to the other extreme, and maintain that the teachings of the Sermon are quite irrelevant to men today. Jesus does not proclaim them as emergency regulations, and certainly Matthew, who probably meant the passage as a conscious echo of the Mosaic morality of Sinai, to emphasize Jesus' Messianic teaching role, wrote them for the use of the continuing Christian Church. Jeremias' theory that they are not moral imperatives at all, but rather indicatives describing life in the Kingdom, seems to ignore the clear fact that, even if a new life is growing in us by God's Spirit, there are definite acts we ought or ought not to perform, as members of the Kingdom. Until we reach perfection, that goal remains a morally obliging ideal. The moral 'ought' cannot be eliminated simply by the expedient of saying that, as members of the Kingdom, we *will* live in a certain way; the fact remains that we actually *ought* to live in that way, whatever means we may use to fulfil our obligations. Finally, the Lutheran view that the Sermon places before us an 'impossible possibility' is not saved from being self-contradictory by the fact that it is apt to sound profound. If it is obligatory, then it is possible; and if it is impossible, then it cannot be obligatory; and that, surely, is that.

It seems to me, then, that the clearest view of the Sermon to take is that, in it, Jesus is sketching graphically and pictorially the sort of attitude which the Christian must always strive to cultivate as far as he can. Just as his reported statement about it being harder for a rich man to enter the Kingdom than for a camel to pass through a needle's eye (Matt. 19.24) is quite clearly not literally true, but an exaggerated, pictorial way of making a point about the dangers of wealth (for, to take just one example, Abraham himself, in whose bosom we are to rest after death, died a very rich man); so Jesus' statements in the Sermon are far from being literal. He is not laying down absurdly difficult or impractical rules, which are to be duties for all men, or for all Christians, or even for some special class of 'religious' Christians. He is setting out the attitudes which characterize the one who takes God as King (the member of the Kingdom), and which will be ideals for him. They are ideals, in that, while morally binding goals of endeavour, they can never be completely achieved, and one's duty is only to seek them as far as one can, in one's own situation. This does not at all make them less important than duties; it means that one cannot judge in advance how far they should be implemented in individual cases; though they remain absolutely binding as general goals of moral effort.

So we are enjoined to seek, as far as we can and in the way that seems most appropriate, the attitudes of peaceableness and reconciliation (Matt. 5.22); of respect for and loyalty to, one's marriage-partner (Matt. 5.28); of absolute honesty (Matt. 5.37); of generosity (Matt. 5.40); and of non-malevolence and impartial love (Matt. 5.44). These are the attitudes which should govern our actions in the world. We pursue them because we see all men as members of the Kingdom of God, under the rule of God, called to perfection and eternal happiness in community with each other. We see that because we ourselves apprehend the being of God, who calls us to response and thereby to our true fulfilment. The virtues of the Sermon on the Mount are theological virtues, because they spring from a vision of humanity as a fellowship under God called to adore and delight in him, and in each other as reflections, images, of his uncreated glory.

Christian morality is a constant pursuit of a fuller realization in oneself of contemplative delight, creative striving, and fellowship with all rational creatures. It is conceivable that a non-Christian could adopt these attitudes and live by the call to perfection which is outlined in the Sermon on the Mount, but the rationale of the Christian view is that men are created for community, dependent co-operation with God's purposes, and delight in God's being. Christian love is primarily a response to the being of God as disclosed in prayer. The theological character of Christian love is given first by the fact that the Christian world-view gives intelligible backing to the pursuit of the interior attitude of reverence, delight, and care, which is the grounding of love. Secondly, Christian love is an attentive response to the being of God, and is directed to rational creatures as images of God's being and independent objects of God's own love. Thirdly, all persons are viewed as called to eternal life, and so they have infinite value and an eternal destiny, in regard to which the circumstances of this earthly life have a decisive significance.

One can thus say that Christian love is grounded in faith, the loving attention to God which elicits our total response, and in hope, the vision of an eternal destiny in which the divine purpose for man can be fulfilled; and it has itself a supernatural dimension, being viewed as a participation by creatures in the very being of God, which is love. This sort of love is a gift of God, which transfigures us into his likeness and unites us ever more closely with himself; its end is the vision of God in the communion of saints, the coming of the Kingdom or Rule of God. Thus the source, the character, and the end of Christian love are rendered distinctive by its integration within a vision of the universe as a purposive expression of the love of God. As long as that fact is borne firmly in mind, then one can say, with Augustine, that love is the only basic Christian principle, and that all the virtues are forms of love.

This completes the analysis of human nature, as seen in a theistic context, for which man is made in the *imago Dei* and called to fulfilment by participating in the love which is God. It may be as well to pause at this point and try to summarize and recapitulate what has been said in chapters 7-11, in a short and systematic form.

It can be said that the foundational principle of Christian morality is the love of God. Such love will include sensitivity and openness to God's being, creative response to him, co-operation in his purposes, and ultimately, a union of reverence and delight. Such love will disclose God as a personal, holy, purposive creator, to whom we respond rightly by co-operating creatively in achieving his purposes in creation. So the analysis of love reveals a subordinate principle included within it, namely: do the will of God; or fulfil the divine purposes. That is certainly part of what loving God must be, though such obedience is always in response to the being of God himself. God's purpose in creation is that creatures should express his glory and share in his love, and so one derives a further basic principle, namely: fulfil the image of God, human nature, in all rational creatures. That principle states what God's purpose in creation is; and from it two further principles are derivable: preserve rational nature; and do not inhibit, contravene, or destroy rational nature. So, given the existence of God and the theological doctrine of his purpose for man (neither of them purely factual matters, it should be said), one can establish a three-fold basic moral principle: do not destroy but preserve and fulfil human nature. From this principle all the general principles of morality, though not every particular moral demand, can be deduced, given a statement of human nature, as intended by God and discernible in empirical facts of human behaviour. The three-fold principle of not harming, preserving, and fulfilling human nature can therefore be specified under the following headings, each representing a main aspect of human nature:

A. SURVIVAL

1. Do not starve, injure or kill.
2. Help those who are sick and hungry.
3. Do what you can to increase the food-supply and maximize security and peace in society.

B. PLEASURE

1. Do not cause pain.
2. Help those in pain.
3. Maximize pleasure and enjoyment and help others in pursuit of their legitimate purposes (those which do not harm others).

C. CULTURE

1. Do not hinder or actively diminish knowledge, art-appreciation, creativity and fellowship; this involves not lying, deceiving, or repressing knowledge.
2. Educate in knowledge, skill, and co-operation.
3. Maximize co-operative cultural pursuits.

D. SPIRITUALITY

1. Do not hinder reverence, dependence, and love, for instance, by intolerance or superstition.
2. Teach prayer and worship, or at least offer to do so.
3. Maximize contemplative love.

Principles A1, B1, C1, and D1 can be formulated as the principle of freedom or non-interference.

A2, B2, C2, and D2 can be formulated as the principle of benevolence, of helping those in need.

A3 and B3 may be construed as the principle of utility or

77

happiness, the pursuit of the greatest happiness of the greatest number.

C3 and D3 may be construed as the principle of self-realization, the perfecting of one's gifts and talents. Thus these principles are all directly derivable from the basic principle of fulfilment.

The principle of fraternity, of co-operation in social action, is a sub-class of C3.

Since many men live together in society, principles of JUSTICE must be added. These seek the maximum of compatible fulfilments, given that men have different abilities and desires. This is a direct inference from the truth that God wills the fulfilment of all his creatures; so we are to seek the fulfilment of all equally. The necessity for social organization gives rise to a number of relevant principles:

1. The principle of equality states that no man is more important than any other, as a man, so all must be considered equally.

2. The principle of fairness states that, where coercion is necessary, there should be balancing benefit and that limited goods should be distributed on criteria of merit or need, except where they accrue by playing in a 'fair game' situation. A 'fair game situation' is one in which, when players are more or less equally matched in skill and starting situation, scarce benefits accrue by a combination of luck and competition. This sort of criterion of distribution, while completely a- (not im-) moral, may be thought desirable in society on grounds of, for example, efficiency or a realistic acceptance of actual human motivations.

3. The principle of liberty states that coercion must be kept to a minimum compatible with the preservation of the principles of freedom and benevolence, and provision of the opportunity of some fulfilment for all (of course, not necessarily the same for each).

4. The principle of legality states that like cases must be treated alike, under a rule of known and open process of legal judgement.

These, then, are the basic principles of morality which are implicit in the Christian doctrine of God as Creator, given that men are cognitive, sensitive, creative, rational, and social beings. Since these principles are implicit in human nature, it can be said that, in general, men can be expected to assent to them when they are explicitly put before them: 'Gentiles who do not possess the Law carry out its precepts by the light of nature ... they display the effect of the law inscribed on their hearts' (Rom. 2.14). In this sense, morality is 'natural' to man. Nevertheless, though one can naturally enough discern the lineaments of God's purposes by reflection upon the nature of his creatures, the Christian attitude to the natural moral law remains distinctive in three main ways.

First, it is *objective*; it is a reflective working out of a basic divine command to fulfil his creatures. This command, in its rigour and inescapability, gives an importance and imperatival character to morality which no account simply in terms of desires or rational prescriptions can do.

Secondly, it is *teleological*; it is founded upon what is taken to be a real purpose in the creation of human being; so its description of what human fulfilment is becomes a statement of the *imago Dei* in man, human nature, not just as it is, but as it is divinely intended. Insight into the divine purpose for man is a foundation of the substantive content of human fulfilment, and it is teleological in a more specific sense: that, from time to time, certain persons feel called to a specific task or vocation, a uniquely individual purpose, which it is their destiny to fulfil. Though it does not come to all, this sense of vocation is very characteristically Christian, and is integrally related to the notion of a Creator who calls one to fulfil a specific purpose to meet some particular need or design. Christian morality is teleological in a third way, too; for it speaks of an eternal destiny for man, in terms of union with God (Heaven) or self-chosen isolation from God (Hell). Consequently, it leads to a view of our daily moral choices which gives them a decisive significance in the shaping of our own natures towards Heaven or Hell.

Thirdly, the Christian view of morality is *attitudinal*; it has its place within the general attitude of openness, creative response, co-operation, and union which is the love of God.

It is this love which discloses the being of God and his purpose; which impels us to do God's will; and which makes Christian morality not only a matter of obedience to principles, but of insight into and response to the being of God as disclosed in the world and human nature. Christian morality is a transformation of the heart to love God and enjoy him for ever, and to do his will out of the joy of his presence. The interpretation of Christian ethics as obedience to an externally imposed set of moral rules totally misses the central point that these rules simply state how, in general, we must act to fulfil his purpose for all creatures, and so to be united with him and all men in eternal love.

12

Authority

In this view of morality there is a clear place for revelation and grace; for where duty is regarded as God's will, this may be specially revealed on particular occasions; and where God is conceived as the creator of all things, he may transform the nature of rational creatures as he wills. But there are various conceptions of how God reveals his will or gives grace to men, and these are relevant to our moral attitudes.

One very simple conception is that God may give specific moral commands at particular times, probably through human vehicles, his 'prophets'. Thus the prophets of the Old Testament related the divine commands—which included killing the Amalekites and abstaining from eels—and Jesus, who was one with the mind of God, issued the moral imperatives of God without error or any imperfection of vision. This is in fact the position I took when I wrote *Ethics and Christianity*; the words of Jesus are morally authoritative because, being one with God he was in the best possible position to know what God's will was. It was theologians, and not philosophers, who pointed out to me the difficulties of this view. There seem to be three major difficulties.

The first difficulty is raised by the development of historical and literary criticism of the biblical documents. Most biblical scholars agree that the Bible gives us an edited collection of sayings and stories culled from oral tradition, brought together for diverse motives and in various ways. Thus one cannot be sure what Jesus meant, by the often isolated and fragmentary sayings which have been edited into collections like the Sermon on the Mount of Matt. 5–7; and indeed one cannot be sure that Jesus himself actually spoke the words attributed to him by a writer many years later, perhaps in order to make some theological point. One's degree of scepticism may be greater or less, but it is certainly true that most biblical scholars would be very hesitant about ascribing, say, the words of John's Gospel to the historical Jesus; and would be even more hesitant about their original context and interpretations. This raises an obvious difficulty for one who might wish to take the recorded words of Jesus as morally authoritative, on the grounds that he actually said them, and that their meaning is fairly clear as it stands.

The second difficulty is raised by changing theological estimates of the nature of the incarnation. On some traditional views (that of Aquinas, for example), Jesus must be taken to have had complete and infallible knowledge, including knowledge of all principles of morality. So his pronouncements on moral questions must be accepted as uttered by an omniscient, truthful, and infallible source. There are, however, alternative accounts of the divinity of Jesus, which can still claim to be fully orthodox, in the sense of conforming to the Chalcedonian definition, but which deny, or at least refrain from asserting, his omniscience and infallibility. Indeed, it would be said that, if one is to take the full humanity of Jesus seriously, one must allow that his knowledge is limited by circumstances of time, place, and education. Perhaps he was even mistaken in thinking that the world was about to come to an end. Though his moral sensitivity and insight into reality must clearly be extraordinarily great, perhaps they had to develop and mature just like any other man's. To the extent that one accepts such a view, the ethical pronouncements attributed to Jesus, while having very great weight, may exhibit obscurities or inadequacies of exposition which undermine any absolute unquestionable authority which some may want to give them.

The third difficulty arises from the great dissatisfaction felt by many theologians with a propositional view of revelation, a view which sees revelation as given in precise verbal formulae. Revelation, it may be said, is an unveiling of the being of God, and takes place primarily through personal encounter. The words in the Bible are simply records by fallible men of such encounters, or memories of them, or even later editorial and literary re-workings of earlier, more direct records. For such a view, the words on the page are only important in so far as they can evoke in the reader something of that first encounter with God which they record. This view of revelation is particularly germane to ethics; for it is well known that Jesus did not in fact promulgate any radically new ethical teaching; all his moral teachings can be paralleled in earlier rabbinical writings. And even if his moral teachings had been new within Judaism, they could all be independently arrived at by independent rational reflection. That is to say, any special moral revelation by Jesus seems rather superfluous, since men could arrive at such moral truths by reason in any case.

It may be said, however, that men do disagree violently about moral issues, so authoritative statements are required to settle such disputes. Furthermore, most men have not got the time, ability or patience to work out ethical principles; so again, a teaching authority could help. As the first Vatican Council put it, the natural law is revealed in order that all may easily, securely and infallibly know the law (Vat. 1, AAS, 42, 562, Denz. 1786). This defence of propositional authority in ethics is, however, patently weak. If men disagree about moral issues, their disagreement is not going to be resolved by an appeal to authority unless they already accept that authority. But one of the main tests of an authority is whether it is morally commendable; Jesus' claim to reveal God would not be at all compelling if he was not judged to be morally good by independent criteria of morality. Since the Christian claim to authority is very widely disputed—partly on moral grounds—it would be of little use in resolving ethical disputes between men in general. Only those people who regard Jesus as morally commendable will accept his authority; and this means that they must have a criterion of moral goodness, independent of revelation. But could he not be an authority at least for those persons who call themselves Christians? The trouble here is that there exist radically different interpretations of

Jesus' teaching—was he a pacifist or communist, for example?—; that he said nothing about major moral problems like abortion or the right to rebel; and that the 'expert moral theologians' appointed by the Church often disagree among themselves, for instance, on the permissibility of contraception. So, while it is true that we might do well to listen to 'moral experts', we cannot simply hand over our moral judgement to them. They themselves disagree and we must reserve the right to disagree conscientiously. Anything else is an abnegation of our responsibility as rational agents; and Christians have always stressed this point by speaking of the 'primacy of conscience'.

If one cannot simply hand over one's conscience to someone else, how then can one appeal to authority in ethics? I think it must be plainly said that one can have only an authority of advice, and never an authority of decision. A man can be a moral authority if he knows more relevant facts; if he has great sensitivity and judgement; if he has practical experience; or if he has greater ability at marshalling and assessing arguments and viewpoints. Then one will be well advised to consult him, and often to follow his guidance in difficult cases. But his arguments must always be open to inspection, and one must remain free to make one's own final decision. Moreover, this sort of authority is always personal, it belongs to the man and not to the office. So the institutionalizing of moral authority is always dangerous and dehumanizing; it is personal qualities which give a man what moral authority he has; no office, whether it be bishop or professor, can of itself confer such authority.

All these considerations count against acceptance of the words of Jesus, as recorded in the Gospels, as morally authoritative in themselves. What one has to say instead is that these words build up a picture of the personality of Jesus as a man of great moral insight; and, more than that, their proper function is to evoke a present disclosure of the living Christ, the mediation of the Divine through the vehicle of this specific personality. Revelation, it will be said, does not consist in the moral principles recorded in the New Testament; those are never original, often maddeningly cryptic, sometimes silly when applied unthinkingly to modern society (as Paul on long hair and women). It consists in the disclosure of God evoked by the records of the apostles' encounter with him in Jesus. It is God who is revealed, not a set of moral principles.

How is this relevant to ethics? It is relevant in four main ways. First, morality has been characterized as obedience to the will of God. This, in turn, has been interpreted not as obedience to a set of principles, but as a reflective, sensitive, and creative response to the being of God as revealed in the world, calling creatures to their fulfilment. For such a view, revelation cannot be distinguished sharply from human insight; the unveiling of God's being which is revelation is the obverse side of the human insight which (itself prompted by grace) discovers God in the world. The Christian tradition treasures a particular series of revelations, given to a specific community, and developing historically to culminate in the complete disclosure of God's nature in Jesus. The one holy and redemptive God who is revealed in that tradition is, Christians naturally believe, the true God; and so it is in the tradition of this community, the Church, that the most adequate disclosure of the nature of God is given. The revelation of God in Jesus is usually held by theologians to be final and unique; not that nothing can ever be added to it, or that we have nothing more to learn, or that truth cannot be found in other religious traditions, but that in the life of Jesus an unalterably true revelation of God was given, in a way which will never be duplicated or superseded. If Christian morality is basically a response to the being of God, then obviously the revelation of God in Christ is of fundamental importance in defining the object to which the believer is concerned to respond. Christian ethics is *revelatory*, in that it is an ethics of response to the God who is disclosed in the Christian tradition. This does not mean that it involves blind obedience to verbal formulae or direct orders from on high. On the contrary, it requires serious reflection and a sustained pursuit of charity and sensitivity to try to discern where the community of faith has indeed preserved the revelatory disclosure of God and

85

where it may have been misled by prejudice and inertia.

Secondly, morality has been construed as a co-operation in the purposes of God. Christian revelation makes the purpose of God clearer: 'He has made known to us in all wisdom and insight the mystery of his will, according to his purpose which he set forth in Christ as a plan for the fulness of time' (Eph. 1.9). In particular, the resurrection is the foundation of the Christian hope of eternal life and of the Christian attitude to personal suffering which sees the possibility of transfiguration even in the ruin of despair. If it is true that human actions are, in general, aimed at the realization of specific purposes, then the disclosure of the divine purpose for men is bound to affect the sorts of action one performs. Indeed, Christianity has often been attacked for being too ascetic or other-worldly; at least such critics see that belief in an eternal destiny for every man will have effects on one's conduct, even if they neglect the strands in Christian thought which call for the establishing of justice and peace in this world, now.

Thirdly, Jesus is taken as an exemplar for Christians, so that Christian ethics is *exemplary*. It is perhaps naive to speak of imitating the historical Jesus, since all we have are four edited documents compiled some time after his death, each with differing theological interests and emphases. Nevertheless in these documents there is discernible the pattern of a certain sort of person, with characteristic virtues, a specific human ideal as represented from four different viewpoints, and this ideal is represented, too, in the annual liturgy of the Church's year. As we move from birth to transfiguration, crucifixion, resurrection, ascension, and Pentecost, so we have dramatically presented the virtues of the Christian ideal: humility, self-giving love, hope, reverence, forgiveness, joy, and peace. Both in liturgy and in the Gospels, we have presented the ideal of human fulfilment which is found in complete response to God. Again, what we are given in revelation is not a set of principles, but a personal ideal, springing from encounter with Jesus himself and dramatically woven around the story of his mission to Israel.

Fourthly, the Christ-ideal does not remain something external, simply to be contemplated or imitated. It is internalized both in the life of the church community and of the individual. The Church is said to be Christ's body and it seeks to manifest the sort of 'sharing love', *koinonia*, which is to characterize the Kingdom of God, those who live under God's rule. There is a specific communal ideal of love, to be realized in Church and family, of trusting, sharing, and tenacious loyalty, which realizes a Christian social ideal. Christ is said to be in the Church, where people gather in his name, so that the eucharist is not only the manifestation of his presence among his people, but the re-creation of his people as 'one body', reconciled and united in him. The conception of the Church as a sacramental community of love, upheld by the presence of Christ as its head, elected to a special mission in the world—to be its light and leaven— gives a special vocational tone to Christian morality which is quite distinctive. Christian morality is *charismatic*, in that it is not simply a pursuit of moral excellence, but seeks to rely on grace, the power of God's love re-creating and renewing human life both in the community and in the individual.

The life of grace is a life of freedom, joy, and spontaneity. It does not contradict obedience to moral principles; in so far as a believer contravenes these principles, he does what is wrong. But just as a happy marriage does not consist simply in following a set of principles for living together, but also in the spontaneous quality of love which does not primarily consider principles; so, in somewhat the same way, while the life of grace will not contravene moral principles, it will transcend them by the quality of its free and joyful loving. This loving grows in the individual as he participates in the life of God, as God works within him to bring love to life. The intense moral seriousness which has been held to characterize Christian morality must be qualified by the consideration that Christian living is also a matter of grace, of the free gift of God's love 'flooding into our hearts', and making us sharers in his love.

For the Christian, God's law is absolute and inexorable in its demands; but obedience to that law is not the arduous, painful, and unrelenting struggle that it may seem. Because

13

The Ten Commandments

There have been a number of controversies in moral theology about the place of rules in Christian ethics. There are those who stand by a set of absolute moral rules—perhaps the Ten Commandments and some principles held to be implied by Natural Law—on abortion, euthanasia, killing, lying, and sexual morality, for example. Then there are those who have espoused what has been called 'situation-ethics', the view, briefly put, that there is only one Christian ethical principle, the rule of love. How does what I have said relate to these issues?

I have said that there is only one foundational principle of Christian morality, though it is a very complicated and obscure one, the love of God. This principle is explicitly theistic, so cannot be identified, for example, with a humanistic understanding of love as respect for persons. Nor can it just be construed by saying, 'Maximize as much love as possible in each situation'. For to understand what the love of God requires is to discern what his purpose in creation is and to co-operate in working out this purpose. Love has to be filled out with an understanding of the *imago Dei* in human nature; that is what must be realized. The content of fulfilled humanity is seen as that distinctive human nature which is willed by God; so one basic moral requirement is the gift of wisdom, of discernment, to see what kind of human good God wills in creation. Love without wisdom is apt to be well-meaning but misguided, but it is equally true that wisdom without practical love is barren and inhuman.

In so far as situation-ethics does not collapse into a form of Utilitarianism, but retains a concern for human good as well as human happiness, then it actually implies principles like those underlying the Ten Commandments. These are principles involved in the attempt to fulfil human nature; one cannot deny them and love. It is instructive to analyse the Ten Commandments, to see what principles do underlie them, and how they should be interpreted by the Christian. This will provide a case-study for the general interpretation and use of ethical injunctions contained in the Bible.

The first commandment—'You shall have no other gods but me'—is addressed to a society for which polytheism is a temptation, and exhorts to belief in the one Covenant-God of Israel. It is thus partly a revelation of the being of God; and the moral exhortation is to be loyal to that revelation. The commandment is not universal; it is addressed to those who have received God's revelation in the Judeo-Christian tradition. It expresses the religious duty of putting God first, the principle of responding fully to God's revelation. So it is a fairly direct expression of a basic moral principle; but its particular form is given by social circumstances (temptation to polytheism), and makes reference to one tradition of divine revelation. In these ways it is particularized.

'You shall not make any idol'; this prohibition is not a direct expression of a moral principle. It is a secondary rule, stating a consequence of believing that God is spirit. So again, it refers to revelation, and prohibits practices which undermine the revelation of God's nature; it prohibits superstition.

'You shall not take the name of the Lord in vain'; this prohibits acts which could undermine reverence for God; it prohibits sacrilege.

'Remember the Sabbath to keep it holy'; the fourth commandment is a secondary rule, a religious regulation intended to preserve the principle of keeping time apart for God (and incidentally of giving workers time off). The positive rules of the Sabbath can certainly not be deduced from moral first principles. They are regulations intended to provide an embodiment of the principle of giving time to worship.

One might systematize this first table of the Law in this

way: given that God has revealed himself, you must respond fully to his revelation; you must do nothing that would undermine the character of that revelation; and you must keep time for teaching and practising worship. These are the three basic moral principles of religion, the principles of not harming, preserving, and fulfilling the spiritual life. The particular formulations of the commandments mention practices which do or could undermine God's revelation: polytheism, idol-worship, and profanation; and one practice is enjoined which is calculated to protect and extend the practice of religion. To apply these commandments today one needs to find corresponding practices which undermine revelation, perhaps materialism, superstition and secularism. The sabbath regulation, which is abrogated for Christians, must be replaced by a personal rule of life which fulfils the same end.

'Honour your father and mother'; the fifth commandment is not a basic principle. It expresses the principle of honouring all men; but it adds to this a duty of special relation. We cannot love all men equally; so we have special obligations to people we are involved with in particular ways: to fellow-workers, members of the Church, parents, and children. We have a special moral concern for our parents; and this is true in a society constituted into families. It could conceivably be different in a non-familial society, where, for instance, children do not know who their own parents are. So this secondary rule depends upon the existence of the institution of the family. It then states that we have a duty of special relation to parents; such duties can, in general, be derived from a statement of the sorts of institutional relationships there are in a given society, which give rise to such special relations. Such duties are not found among the first principles of morality. As far as that goes, any institutions are permissible which do not contravene such principles. But, given such institutionalized relations—which must exist, in some form, in every society—special responsibilities accrue in virtue of them. This commandment states one of them, which accrues in one possible form of social organization of relations. A corresponding secondary rule could be found for societies which have different sets of relations; where there is tribal grouping, for example ('Honour the tribal elders' might do).

'You shall not kill'; this is a clear first principle, prohibiting the infliction of harm on others (or oneself). It is one direct deduction from the general principle of non-interference.

'You shall not commit adultery'; the seventh commandment is not a basic principle. It derives from the principles of not causing harm to others and of not dishonouring the human person in oneself and others. This formulation of the principles presupposes the institution of marriage and prohibits acts undermining that institution. In all societies there must be some form of regulating sexual relationships, so a corresponding general principle would be, not to undermine whatever regulations there are in this matter. The reason for that would be that it would cause harm, either immediately to an injured party or indirectly by weakening the institution. There are further considerations here of the role of sexuality in personal relationships; and a more positive formulation might be: preserve the marriage-bond, a life-long commitment of persons in trust to each other.

Although marriage is not an institution deducible from moral first principles, it has a central place in the Christian tradition, and it may be thought to be hallowed by revelation (in our Lord's teaching, for example). In any case, it is an institution calculated to preserve and extend the moral principle of cultivating personal relationships of a fulfilling sort. In this respect, its status is rather like that of the sabbath regulations. It is not the only possibility; but it has become part of the revealed tradition, part of the norm of Christian living. So this is a secondary rule, arising from the institution of life-long monogamy; but that institution may itself be valued as a revelation and expression of the mystery of the union of Christ and his Church, God and his people.

'You shall not steal'; another fairly direct deduction from the principle of non-interference. People feel this to be complicated, when they do, because in some circumstances a society may be so unjust in distributing its goods that such unfairness may be thought to outweigh the prohibition on taking another's possessions (as in the compulsory purchase of land or nationalization of means of production).

'You shall not bear false witness'; this is a direct deduction from first principles, prohibiting false accusations against others. It derives from the principles of non-interference and fraternity. The basic reason why one should not lie is that to do so undermines trust between men; and such trust is a condition of building up a body of knowledge or of co-operating in creative activities. So it is directly ruled out by the obligation to maximize knowledge and creative co-operation.

'You shall not covet'; the tenth commandment is unusual in referring to attitudes, not just actions. It prohibits the attitude of envy, which may lead to stealing. So it simply carries out the process of interiorizing the eighth commandment in a way that Jesus explicitly did in the 'sermon on the mount'; it thus makes the point that morality is concerned with one's attitudes of mind as well as with one's acts—or, at least religious morality is so concerned.

Of these latter six commandments, three are direct applications of moral first principles of non-interference and social self-realization; one explicitly relates the commands to attitudes as well as acts; and two are concerned with preserving the institution of the family, an institution which may be seen as revealed by God. It is clear that one cannot find in this list a systematic exposition of basic Christian or Jewish principles. It must be remembered that this is only a minute part of the Torah, which Jews take to be the revealed Law of God for his people. The Christian attitude to 'revealed law' is more ambiguous. The Law is abrogated clearly in Romans 7.4, and Christians do not keep the Old Testament food laws. Yet Jesus came to fulfil the Law, and the Sermon on the Mount gives a sort of Christian Torah. One can see how readily disputes and difficulties will arise. Some will take every particular injunction to be divinely commanded, even to keeping the Sabbath (I do not, however, know of any Christians who do this consistently, and keep the whole Torah in its entirety). Some will take every secondary injunction to be abrogated, leaving only a set of primary moral principles. Thus commands four, five, and seven would be replaced in practice by corresponding principles of making time for God, doing (unspecified) duties of special relation, and preserving whatever personally fulfilling institutions of sexual regulation might be found in specific and changing societies. Yet others might retain four, five, and seven (replacing Sabbath by Lord's day), in the belief that the institutions of a holy day and of the family are divinely revealed, though specific forms of observance may change.

As far as morality goes, secondary rules are permissible, as long as they do not contradict a basic moral principle; if they do, they must be ignored. And in general, they should be seen to help in the accomplishment of some end itself enjoined by primary principles, or in avoiding breaking such principles. One could recommend food laws on the ground that they remind the believer of his setting-apart by God; or the institution of marriage on the ground that it implements family care and mutual love in a distinctive and valuable way. But disputes will inevitably arise in this area, as indeed they did in the early Church. Clearly, some secondary rules are necessary to social life. But the Christian must distinguish clearly between primary and secondary rules, and always be prepared to adapt secondary rules in view of changing circumstances; whereas the primary principles are unchangeable, being based on the nature of man in general. Further than that, it will clearly be best if Christians decide to live with their differences and accept that some can take secondary moral principles more seriously than others, without this causing the sort of absolute moral breakdown which occurs when primary moral rules are denied. In the case of secondary moral principles, people who take differing interpretations may live together in tolerance, as long as each accepts the honesty and good-will of the other.

This analysis of the Ten Commandments has provided a very wide interpretation. Taken literally, the list merely excludes polytheism, idol-worship, blasphemy, killing, stealing, adultery, false accusations, and coveting, and enjoins respect for parents and sabbath-observance. This would leave them very limited in application, fairly easy to keep, and lacking in moral principles like benevolence and self-realization. No doubt this code of laws was intended for a primitive society, and thus primarily applies to a situation with which we will never be confronted. But it is reasonable to suppose that one may find, behind the specific commands, more general presupposed norms which do make a claim upon one. In seeking to formulate these more general principles, there is much room for diverse interpretations. For even the person who expects to find in the Bible a consistent web of ethical principles, all of which make some claim upon one, must undertake a difficult and judicious weighing of various texts against each other. For instance, one must balance 'respect for parents' against Jesus' hard words about hating one's father and mother for his sake; neither can simply be ignored. For one who holds that the perception of God's activity and its ethical consequences is often fragmentary and imperfect, sometimes mistaken, throughout the biblical records, one's canon of interpretation must come from elsewhere. Perhaps it will be in the general tradition of the Church or the paradigm of Jesus' death and resurrection, which enables him to build up an overall pattern among the biblical texts, giving some parts more weight than others (for instance, Jesus' recorded words more weight than Jeremiah's), and perhaps rejecting some (for instance, Deuteronomy 20) as quite unacceptable. The former interpreter will often be tempted to strain a text to breaking-point to get some contemporary application out of it; while the latter will be tempted to discard uncomfortable, but perhaps salutary, elements of the tradition without due consideration.

There is, then, an ineradicable possibility of divergent interpretation of all biblical rules, including the Ten Commandments. That it should be so is, as I have already argued, part of what it means to be fully human, so that the exercise of judgement is an essential part of our humanity. When Calvin treated the Ten Commandments in volume 2 of the *Institutes*, he took them to enjoin obedience to all authorities; the preservation of life by all possible means; measure and modesty in marriage; and to prohibit

14

Moral Rules

The sort of ethical theory which holds that moral rules are no more than convenient rules of thumb has become known as 'situation-ethics'. On this theory, the whole idea of a set of moral rules sometimes seems to be rejected: 'There can never be a system of Christian ethics', writes Joseph Fletcher in his book, *Situation Ethics*. Fletcher's case is that moral decisions must be made situationally; this means that one must take care to know all the facts; one must calculate consequences; and then one must decide to do whatever realizes 'more good (loving-kindness)' than any other alternative. 'Love is compelled to be calculating, careful, prudent, distributive.'

Of course, morality should never be considered as the automatic application of moral rules, without prudence and love. But the function of moral principles is just to say what loving action consists in, in general types of case, not killing, stealing, lying and so on. Fletcher says that 'ethical maxims are illuminators'; but this misses the point that killing, for instance, is incompatible with loving, and so its prohibition is a definite rule, not just an illuminator. By denying rules, Fletcher seems to be denying that any acts, as such, are incompatible with love; but that view is surely untenable; for if we know what love is, there must be types of act which are loving and other types which are not; then the specification of these will provide our ethical system.

Situation-ethics is misleading at another point, too. Fletcher holds that there are no values; something 'is a value because somebody decided it was worth something'. Love then consists simply in satisfying men's needs and purposes, whatever they are. This appears to be a form of the Benthamite Utilitarianism which Mill rejected (albeit ambiguously). One may wonder why Fletcher allows love to be an intrinsic good, rather than consistently making it one of the things men may want or need. More to the point, one may wish to reject the view that values are the results of human decision, on the grounds that God decrees what is really of value, and sets the *imago Dei* as an objective ideal for men. There are values in objective reality; these outline the sort of character men ought to have, whatever they may in fact want or like. Christian morality is not only concerned with helping others to get what they like. It is primarily concerned with the development of knowledge and creativity, both in oneself and others. It is this positive ideal of human fulfil-ment which seems to be missing from Fletcher's view of Christian ethics.

Situation-ethics tries to reduce morality to just one prin-ciple, that of love. That can in a sense be done. But then one must build so much into the concept of 'love' that it may well be thought clearer to have a number of principles—justice, prudence, benevolence, freedom, fulfilment, and so on—which make clear what love must be, when applied to the human situation. Moreover, it must be remembered that the Christian may find many uniquely vocational moral demands made upon him which are not deducible from one general principle together with factual information alone. In this respect, too, it is unrealistic to suppose that there is just one ethical principle from which all particular duties can be deduced. One may say that it is true that no moral obligation can conflict with the principle of love—one can ensure this by defining 'loving activity' as synonymous with 'what one ought to do'. But such a very general principle is unlikely to specify particular duties, in the complexity of human life. Rules of the sort outlined in chapter 11 are necessary to show what love consists in; and even they are too general to be simply applied to situations as they come up. Moral decision-making is not just a question of apply-ing one, or even many rules; it is a question of formulating new rules or modifications of existing rules to fit new situa-tions. Nor can such rules be merely rules of thumb, in the sense that they are rough-and-ready guides which may be replaced if more efficient means to achieving one's purposes are found. For they attempt to state what ought to be done, and thus they place limits on permissible purposes. They do not state morally neutral means to an independent end; they state the sorts of act which are morally permissible or obligatory in a certain situation; so we are not free to modify or ignore them at will.

Moral rules can, of course, be modified and often need to be. For the situations they are meant to apply to may change; or we may find that they were inadequately thought out to start with; or two or more moral rules may conflict. Fletcher puts the case misleadingly again when he holds that moral rules—like not lying—can be overruled by love. In fact, any moral principle may be overruled by another moral principle, in a given situation. It is very easy to think of a situation in which two moral principles conflict; and in such a case one of them must be abrogated. For instance, it is a duty to help, or not to harm, others. It is also a duty not to lie. But if telling the truth will cause great and irreparable harm to another, one may be justified in lying— or so most people would say. If one does tell the truth, then one breaks the rule of not harming others, which is at least as strong a principle. Either way, some moral principle must be broken; there is no easy way out. This establishes that moral principles cannot be absolute, in the sense of unbreakable for any reason. But they are still morally binding, where there is no conflicting moral rule. A moral principle can only be overruled by another moral principle; but one cannot say that there is a clear and absolute order of priority among moral principles, such that one will always overrule the other in a given situation.

One can, perhaps, construct a sort of table of precedence of moral principles in general. Priority goes to those rules prohibiting the taking of life; for murder deprives a man of any condition of fulfilment. Second are the duties of non-interference and non-malevolence, the prohibition of causing pain—though the gravity of the rule is proportional to the intensity of the pain to be incurred. Third is the duty of

benevolence, of helping the needy and preserving what I
have called minimal rights; and again, the duty is more
binding, the greater the need of the sick or deprived person.
Fourth is the duty of providing the conditions of positive
freedom, of growth in knowledge and creative action. Fifth
is the duty of helping others to pursue their legitimate aims;
and sixth is the duty of maximizing knowledge, culture, and
love, the fulness of the *imago Dei*. The duties of justice—
equality and fairness—are concerned with the distribution
of other duties, and so apply throughout the table.

In general, perfect prohibitive duties (those which prohibit
an act and allow no exceptions on grounds of inclination)
are stronger than positive imperfect duties of preservation
(duties enjoining acts preserving the conditions of fulfilment,
allowing exceptions); and these are stronger than imperfect
positive duties of fulfilment, in cases of conflict. This is
because the fulfilment of human nature presupposes its
preservation, which in turn presupposes that it is not
destroyed. The first priority rules are those which are presupposed by the rules of lower priority—though, of course,
the rules of 'low priority' really provide the *raison d'être* for
moral effort at all, and without them the other duties might
well collapse to a great extent.

When one is weighing various moral rules against one
another, in a specific situation, one also needs to take into
account the degrees of harm or help, the number of persons
involved, and the length of time involved. These factors are
fairly obvious, in that it is worse to impede or prevent the
possibility of someone's fulfilment than positively to aid
someone else's fulfilment, if such a straight choice must be
made. The fact is, of course, that a straight choice is rarely
involved, so matters become a very complicated question
of balancing many impalpable considerations and consequences. This calls for great skill and judgement, and a
simple appeal to rules is of no avail. Most of the moral
dilemmas which arise today consist in conflicts of many
moral principles which have consequences very difficult to
discern. We may wish for a firm rule to give certitude; but
that is simply a failure of moral understanding and a lack

of moral sensitivity. It is not because we do not care; it is precisely because we care intensely, that we must often refuse to offer crude certainties where the appropriate, if agonizing, method is one of seeking wisdom and love in balancing diverse moral principles in particular cases. It is most important for Christians to realize that to try to apply a set of moral rules rigidly and absolutely is in fact an immoral procedure, demonstrating a lack of sensitivity and rationality. It is no doubt this sort of thing that people like Fletcher were reacting against in propounding 'situation-ethics'. But moral sensitivity does not require us to give up moral rules altogether; it simply requires us to admit that human situations are extremely complex, that there are many moral rules which often conflict, and that careful judgement is required in assessing and balancing these factors in particular cases. Christian morality does need rules or principles; but Christians are not moral computers, applying the rules according to clear and defined formulae. They are human beings, using judgement and sensitivity in particular cases to decide how the rules are to be applied to achieve the greatest human fulfilment.

The view I have outlined might very well be called a Natural Law theory, since it elaborates a set of basic moral principles by reasoned consideration of human nature; and it grounds those principles in the eternal law of God for man, the *imago Dei*. I do not mind that appellation, though I doubt whether it is very helpful, for so many different things go by the name of Natural Law. In particular, I would want to make it clear that this is not a naturalistic theory—a theory which founds morality simply on facts about human nature, or which asserts that nature's purposes, whatever they are, should not be impeded. For the very conception of human nature on which it builds is the notion of an ideal nature, the *imago Dei*, which is commanded by God, and in accordance with which actual nature must be shaped by man's free action; so it is explicitly non-naturalistic. Nor does this view found morality solely upon the contingent fact of human desires, though of course desires are important to any ethical theory. On the contrary, it retains and stresses an element of absolute categorical obligation, a feature which has often been lacking in presentations of traditional Natural Law views.

Secondly, it is not legalistic, demanding strict conformity to specific detailed principles. It does set before men prohibitions and ideals, but the precise point of these is to make room for creative advance and free choice of purposes within a harmonious society. Thirdly, though I would expect most rational men to accept most of the principles outlined, positive conceptions of human fulfilment may well differ, especially in view of Christian belief in eternal life by relation to a transcendent God. The principles of moral law are founded on the notion of God as creator; those who do not accept such a doctrine, or who may have a different conception of his purpose for mankind, cannot be expected to agree with all that has been said. Indeed, I have been at pains to point out the distinctive features of a Christian view of morality. One would expect those who wish to construct a rational morality to be concerned for survival, pleasure and some aspects of culture at least. One might expect differences on the question of whether there is some one ideal for man as such (a Christian would say, the love of God in the fellowship of others); humanists would be more likely to speak of many permissible ideals, none of them demanded of men, and of morality as a more restricted business of maintaining the conditions of a tolerable human social existence. Again, humanists may speak of moral principles as giving reasons for action, but not necessarily overwhelming reasons; perhaps, they may say, other reasons (for example, artistic ones) may predominate; or perhaps one just does not want to be moral, on occasion at least. Whereas a Christian, seeing the moral law in terms of God's command, would find moral reasons overwhelmingly strong, and to be followed, not because and in so far as one wants to ameliorate the human condition, but because one ought to respond to God fully and unreservedly. Finally, but most important, Christians see the moral life as just part of the pursuit of the love of God, and indeed the participation in that love, at the level of human relationships. This supernatural or mystical strain in Christian morality must not be lost sight of; it is, after all, what gives point to the Christian life and, a Christian would say, to the existence of created beings.

15

Summary

For the Christian, morality is not simply a matter of decision, or of having certain feelings, or of integrating and maximizing desires; it is a matter of what God wills, by the inner necessity of his being as one whose unchangeable nature it is to love. A philosophical justification of this was undertaken in *Ethics and Christianity*, which no doubt is rather hard going; and I have not tried to reproduce it here. It may be in place, however, to recall very briefly the outline of my argument in that book, and relate it to some of the things that have been said here.

I began by arguing that ethics is objective, which means that true moral propositions must be made true by moral facts. That is, if 'P ought to do X' is true, what makes it true is the existence of a certain fact. There is, I claimed, only one moral fact, which is the being of God; for God is the reality which makes all true moral assertions true. I sometimes called God the moral demand, or the Ideal of the Good, construing this as a unitary reality which demands various attitudinal responses from men. These demanded attitudes comprise the virtues, and each virtue is a response to some aspect of the Ideal. What God wills is the fulfilment of human nature, the realization of the *imago Dei* in man. This *imago Dei* is the ideal human nature; and the various aspects of this ideal constitute what may be called a realm of values. Values are exemplary archetypes of human possibilities; they provide the content of the *imago Dei*, the content of God's will for creation. Values are timeless and eternal, but they give rise to moral claims at specific times, binding particular men to pursue fulfilment in specific ways. Such claims may or may not be consciously experienced;

104

they are the actual obligations which men have at particular times, as a result of the relation of values to particular states of affairs; and those values are in turn aspects of the *imago Dei*, which states the will of God for creation. So, though it may sound as though there are many disparate moral claims, values, and virtues, they are all ultimately aspects of one unitary reality, construed as the will of God, the objective purpose which is morally binding on men. One may thus speak of moral facts in the plural, when thinking of the specific claims binding on men; or of moral fact in the singular, when stressing that these claims arise from the one will of God willing the one thing, fulfilment of the *imago Dei*.

That course of argument was intended to show how duty can be identical with the will of God, construed as the moral fact which makes moral propositions true or false. I have followed the subsequent arguments of *Ethics and Christianity*, taking Christian morality to be *objective*, in being founded upon an objective moral claim, the being of God; *attitudinal*, in requiring the pursuit of specific interior attitudes; and *teleological*, in three ways—in presupposing a purposive ordering of human nature; in giving rise to vocational demands on some occasions; and in setting an ultimate goal for human endeavour in the vision of God beyond death.

I have modified the account in two respects. In speaking of the *charismatic* nature of Christian morality, its reliance on grace, I have stressed the communal element more; the way in which the Church is called to be the community of grace, sharing love together in the power of the Spirit; and I have provided quite a different account of that character which I called 'authoritative'. I have here characterized Christian morality as *revelatory*—arising in a particular tradition of response to God—and as *exemplary*, maintaining an ideal pattern of life, based on the paradigm revelatory event of Jesus. I would still wish to relate Christian morality in some essential way to Christian revelation, but to leave open the possibility of a wider understanding of authority than that which relies on the *ipsissima verba* of

Jesus or the Bible. My purpose has not in any way been to replace a 'conservative' by a 'liberal' theology, but to develop an account of authority in Christian ethics which might be common ground between diverse traditions of interpretation.

In this book, I have basically tried to provide an account of what it means to understand one's duty as the will of God, and in particular to show how this does not involve an infantile acceptance of authority, but does involve reflection, judgement, and insight; sensitivity and a creative exercise of freedom; and a concern for human fulfilment in a just society. If I had to choose one phrase with which to characterize the Christian's moral outlook, that phrase would be: 'creative response'. One must respond to the moral claims of one's situation, but one must do so by the exercise of spontaneous and creative freedom; the moral life largely consists in the skilful balancing of these two factors of freedom and response. I have tried to show how the general principles of morality can be worked out by reflection on the conditions of human existence, as the existence of a creature of God, and I have outlined what those principles are. I have suggested how Christian decision-making in ethics, while it remains decision-making, calling for rationality and practical wisdom, takes place in a context of response to the God revealed in Christ and of growth into the ideal of the Christ-life within the sacramental community of the Church. Thus I have attempted to answer the three questions I posed at the outset; of what one means by saying that something is right or wrong; of what sorts of things are right or wrong; and of how one decides whether something is right or wrong.

I have not dealt with the difficult doctrines of sin, the fall, and redemption; and with the way in which these complicate the application of the general moral principles I have outlined. Nor have I given detailed applications of these principles to specific moral problems. Those topics need to be, and I hope will be, treated separately. I have simply tried to expound what it can mean to interpret morality in terms of obedience to the will of God and so to expound a distinctively Christian view of morality which I think is intrinsically worth commending. This does not constitute a 'proof of God' in any sense; it is an exploration of the sort of moral attitudes which would seem appropriate to one who already accepts a Christian doctrine of God. One may see morality in terms of over-riding claims, as rooted in objective reality, as enjoining the pursuit of a personal ideal, as concerned with interior attitudes as well as with actions, as involving vocational or quasi-purposive demands, and as pointing to a need to find some way of coming to terms with moral failure and guilt. To the extent that one sees morality in these ways, a theistic interpretation of morality will seem natural; and so these may come to form elements in the construction of a theistic view of the world. But of course, consideration of other things than morality is necessary in providing a justification of belief in God. My concern has been limited to sketching a Christian view of morality; and secondarily, to commending such a view, not as compellingly obvious, but as intelligible in itself and as embodying a mature, adequate, reflective and sensitive response to those features of human existence with which morality is concerned.

Appendix: Duty and the Will of God

Many objections have been raised to the formulation that 'X is right' means 'God wills X'. Nevertheless, I regard it as defensible, despite the difficulties involved in the concepts of synonymy, meaning, and identity, which make some chary of using these notions at all. Exponents of what has been called the autonomy of ethics have wished to say that central moral notions such as 'ought', 'good', and 'right' are not reducible to or derivable from non-moral concepts or justifiable by appeal to non-moral reasons. If there is a God, they maintain, his existence is irrelevant to morality (except in so far as he is the remote cause of everything in the universe). Moral standards are independent of God; indeed, God is himself assessed as 'good' in terms of them. The difficulty with this view—and it seems insuperable—is that for a theist, God is the creator of all things, including morality; therefore morality cannot be independent of God, much less an external standard by which he can be assessed. Consequently, some theists, who may be called theological naturalists, have held that moral obligations are based wholly on the purpose and power of God, so that morality depends on religion, and has no independent existence or justification. 'God's willing X' provides a reason, the only adequate reason, for doing X (where X is a possible human act); and moral obligation could not be taken so seriously, or at all, without belief in God. The objection to this view is that it seems to make God an amoral tyrant, not worthy of adoration; and this objection too seems insuperable. So the problem is this: how can God be both worthy of worship in himself and the creator of moral standards?

My proposal is this: God does create the moral law, but

not arbitrarily or contingently. It is founded on his immutable purpose for his creation; and true moral values are finite images of his own necessary being and perfection. The standard of goodness is the necessary and immutable perfection of God's own being. It is in this sense that 'X is right' means 'God wills X'. According to this proposal (it could be termed the identity thesis), moral obligations are not being reduced to (analysed wholly in terms of) non-moral facts. Rather, it is being said that the fact that God is what he is, is not a fact which can be expressed in morally neutral terms; the Divine claim on creatures cannot be reduced to a contingent command or request; the quality of inexponable and categorical obligation remains. Indeed, it is precisely the being of God, the source of moral claims upon creatures, which safeguards the objective reality of human moral standards. Of course, moral obligations can be understood and accepted without belief in God. However, this does not mean that obligations and the being of God are logically independent. One can in general believe X without believing Y, or even while denying Y, even though X is identical with Y. For instance, one can believe that a flash of lightning occurs, and deny that an electrical discharge has occurred, even though a lightning flash is identical with an electrical discharge in the atmosphere. An atheist clearly will not recognize moral obligations under the description of 'Divine claims', since he denies the existence of God. Nevertheless, when a theist says, 'I ought to do X', he may intend to mean 'God wills X'; and, he will say, not only does *he* mean it thus, but his statement actually does mean that (for it describes a situation which is identical with a situation correctly and more comprehensively described as 'God wills X'). It follows that 'God wills X' cannot be a reason for 'You ought to do X', since they state the identical state of affairs under different descriptions. Thus 'Do X because God wills it' does not justify a moral obligation in non-moral terms; similarly, 'You ought to do God's will' is a tautology, like 'You ought to do your duty', which may nonetheless often have a significant use—for instance, as a sort of reminder of the seriousness of moral obligation.

110

However, though belief in God does not justify moral belief, in that morality would be unjustifiable without belief in God, it could be said to justify morality in that theism provides a picture of a changeless, objective being making absolute claims and promising final fulfilment, so that categorical obligations have an intelligible placing in the universe. Theism gives a reason for being moral, in the sense of providing an overall pattern, making wider connections, giving a metaphysical context; not in the sense of providing non-moral or prudential motives (in terms of God's power, or Heaven and Hell). The provision of such a wider context helps to support a particular way of seeing moral obligations (as unconditional yet related to human good) which could perhaps be undermined by metaphysical arguments.

Because the introduction of the concept of 'God' introduces such wider considerations, one will not wish to say that 'God wills X' means the same as 'You ought to do X' (even where X is a possible human act) *tout court*. It may be better to follow Frege in distinguishing meaning and reference, and to say, in the formulation introduced above, that 'X is right' refers to a situation identical with that, more comprehensively described as 'God willing X'. But there is an intelligible sense of 'means' in which to say this can be expressed by the phrase, 'when P says that X is right, he means that God wills X'.

For these reasons neither the theist nor the atheist can morally assess God, so the 'open question' argument, which is the chief support of the so-called Naturalistic Fallacy (in this case, the alleged mistake of defining 'good' in terms of God's will), fails of application. The theist cannot logically ask, 'Is God good?', since he defines God as the standard of goodness. The atheist cannot ask the question, since he denies the existence of God; he can only ask, self-defeatingly, whether a being, X, is commendable enough to be really God. It is thus not an open question, whether God is good. When one says, 'God is good', one means (in part at least) that the perfections of God's being define what it is to be good. One may also mean that God acts to help creatures to conform to the fulness of the divine image. This raises the

111

problem of how God can both be a standard of goodness and an agent who acts in specific ways, governed only by his own nature. But that is a separate problem, to which there is, I believe, an adequate solution. In any case, one does not mean that God is morally good (as if he could be bad). One adores the necessary goodness of God; one does not commend his worthy moral efforts.

I propose, then, that morality is epistemologically independent of God, but ontologically dependent. If there is a God, his being determines what is morally right or wrong; it is God one meets in being morally obliged, though the atheist may fail to see him. In this sense, the theist is bound to say that when he holds something to be morally right, he means that God wills it.

Bibliography

Good general introductions to ethics are: Frankena, *Ethics* (Prentice-Hall, 1965) and J. Hospers, *Human Conduct* (Hart-Davis, 1963).

Source material for Christian ethics is to be found in: W. Beach and H. R. Niebuhr, eds., *Christian Ethics: Sources of the Living Tradition* (Ronald Press, New York, 1973); and the Anglican handbook *Teaching Christian Ethics* (SCM, 1974) contains extensive bibliographies. J. MacQuarrie, ed., *A Dictionary of Christian Ethics* (SCM, 1967) is useful; and LeRoy Long, *A Survey of Christian Ethics* (OUP, 1967) is well worth consulting.

On duty and God's will, see the papers in part 3 of I. T. Ramsey, ed., *Christian Ethics and Contemporary Philosophy* (SCM, 1966), esp. P. H. Nowell-Smith, *Morality: Religious and Secular*. Also, R. W. Hepburn, *Christianity and Paradox*, ch. 8 (Watts, 1958); and W. W. Bartley, *Morality and Religion* (Macmillan, 1971).

On Natural Law, the classic text is A. P. D'Entrèves, *Natural Law* (Hutchinson, 1951); see also H. L. A. Hart, *The Concept of Law*, ch. 9 (OUP, 1961); I. T. Ramsey, 'Towards a Rehabilitation of Natural Law' in *Christian Ethics and Contemporary Philosophy*; and J. MacQuarrie, *Three Issues in Ethics* (SCM, 1970). The relevant part of Aquinas is the *Summa Theologiae*, 2,1; qus. 90–4.

For the Thomist concept of God, see Aquinas, *Summa Theologiae* 1,1; qus. 1–26. A Lutheran view of Natural Law can be found in H. Thielicke, *Theological Ethics* 1, chs. 19–21 (A. and C. Black, 1968). For Barth's position, see *Church Dogmatics* 2,2, pp. 517 ff (T. and T. Clark, 1957). For some material on Process-theology, see Hartshorne, *Creative Syn-*

113

thesis and Philosophical Method (SCM, 1970).

For material on 'moral seriousness' and opposed views, see G. Wallace and A. D. M. Walker, eds., *The Definition of Morality* (Methuen, 1970). On ethical objectivity, see R. M. Hare, *The Language of Morals* (OUP, 1952); and Iris Murdoch, *The Sovereignty of the Good* (Routledge and Kegan Paul, 1970). For Kant, see the author's *The Development of Kant's View of Ethics* (Basil Blackwell, 1972) and Immanuel Kant, *The Doctrine of Virtue* (Harper Torchbooks, 1964). On the cardinal virtues, see R. C. Mortimer, *Elements of Moral Theology* (A. and C. Black, 1947). Other books relevant to ethical objectivity are G. E. Moore, *Principia Ethica* (OUP, 1903); W. D. Ross, *The Right and the Good* (Clarendon, 1930) and R. S. Downie and E. Telfer, *Respect for Persons* (Allen and Unwin, 1969). For an opposing view to ethical personalism, see W. G. Maclagan, *The Theological Frontiers of Ethics* (Allen and Unwin, 1961).

On the final end of man, Aristotle's *Nicomachean Ethics* is a standard text. Kenneth Kirk, *The Vision of God* (Longmans Green, 1931) presents an Anglican Catholic view; for a Protestant reaction, see Emil Brunner, *The Divine Imperative* (Lutterworth, 1937); for a sensitive treatment of 'original sin' and the 'fall', see Tennant, *The Origin and Propagation of Sin* (OUP, 1902).

On duties of survival, see A. G. N. Flew, *Evolutionary Ethics* (Macmillan, 1968). A sensitive treatment of sexual ethics is in R. Atkinson, *Sexual Morality* (Hutchinson, 1965); and a discussion worth noting is P. Harris *et al.*, *On Human Life: an examination of Humanae Vitae* (Burns and Oates, 1968). On aggression, see P. Ramsey, *The Just War* (Scribners, 1968); Ramsey's book *Basic Christian Ethics* (SCM, 1953) is worth looking at in general. There are relevant papers, too, in R. Preston, *Technology and Social Justice* (SCM, 1971).

On duties of pleasure, see the discussion on Utilitarianism in P. Foot, *Theories of Ethics* (OUP, 1967); of course, J. S. Mill, *Utilitarianism* (many editions); and T. K. Hearn, ed., *Studies in Utilitarianism* (Meredith, New York, 1971).

On duties of justice, two wide-ranging discussions are:

J. Rawls, *A Theory of Justice* (OUP, 1972) and S. I. Benn and R. S. Peters, *Social Principles and the Democratic State* (Allen and Unwin, 1959). M. Cranston, *What Are Human Rights?* (1973) is also worth reading.

On New Testament ethics, see J. Jeremias, *The Sermon on the Mount* (Athlone Press, 1961); W. D. Davies, *The Setting of the Sermon on the Mount* (OUP, 1964); and J. L. Houlden, *Ethics and the New Testament* (Pelican, 1973).

On authority, see Aquinas, *Summa Theologiae*, qu. 79, arts. 12, 13. Also Hastings Rashdall, *Theory of Good and Evil*, bk 2, vol. 2, ch. 5 (OUP, 1907). The papers on the use of the Bible in the periodical *Theology*, March-April 1973, may be useful. A conservative view is in the author's *Ethics and Christianity* (Allen and Unwin, 1970), part 2.

On moral rules and related issues, see J. Fletcher, *Situation Ethics* (SCM, 1966); G. R. Dunstan, *The Artifice of Ethics* (SCM, 1974) and Helen Oppenheimer, *Law and Love* (Faith Press, 1962). Augustine's famous remarks about love can be found in *Homilies on 1 John*, in *Augustine's Later Works*, ed., J. Burnaby (Library of Christian Classics, vol. 8, SCM, 1955) and in *The City of God*, chs. 10 and 19. Calvin on the Ten Commandments is in *Institutes of the Christian Religion*, 2, 8, ed., J. T. McNeill (Library of Christian Classics, vol. 22, SCM, 1961). A book worth noting is R. H. Charles, *The Decalogue* (T. and T. Clark, 1923); see also, *Christian Ethics and Contemporary Philosophy*, part 4.